Too Good to be False is almost too good to be true! This book takes a fresh look at the uniquely great character of Jesus, and finds in his greatness a new and compelling case for the truth of his story as presented in the Gospels. If you think there are no surprises left to be found in his life, prepare to be surprised yourself by this remarkable new book.

Josh McDowell, best-selling author and speaker

In this engaging and exhilarating book, Tom Gilson breathes new life into an old premise: that Jesus was more than just an ordinary rabbi with special effects, but his awe-inspiring character and teachings point persuasively toward his divine nature. In a breezy style, Tom makes the compelling case that Jesus couldn't possibly be the product of mere legends because he is quite literally too good *not* to be true. This might be the most surprising and refreshing book you'll read this year!

Lee Strobel, *New York Times* best-selling author,
director of The Strobel Center at Colorado Christian University

Too Good to be False takes a fascinating look at the human character of Jesus, uncovering fresh insights for believers and skeptics to see that Jesus' story is not simply a story—it's truly, truly too good to be false.

Eric Metaxas, #1 *New York Times* bestselling author and
host of the nationally syndicated *Eric Metaxas Radio Show*

This book is an absolute delight to read and it wonderfully fills a big hole in contemporary apologetics. While it revives an older argument that has dropped out of the contemporary scene, it updates and exposes that argument in a fresh way. Its brilliance lies in the approach of arguing for Jesus' uniqueness and Deity based on what Jesus *did not* do. I have never approached the gospels in this way and, with Gilson's guidance, I have come to love, respect, and worship Jesus with renewed vigor and insight. Honestly, this book must be in your library. I am grateful that it is available to a new generation who will be strengthened and equipped by its argumentation.

JP Moreland, Distinguished Professor of Philosophy, Talbot School of
Theology, Biola University and author of *Scientism and Secularism*

Tom Gilson has written a splendid book that takes us on a wonderful journey to see Jesus with fresh eyes! Gilson distills for us a riveting picture of Christ's virtuous character, his commanding authority, his rigorous intellect, and his beautiful selflessness. This book reveals just why this Man from Nazareth is both the compelling and incomparable historical figure that he is.

Paul Copan, Pledger Family Chair of Philosophy and Ethics, Palm Beach
Atlantic University, and author of *A Little Book for New Philosophers*

I may never before have made this comment in a recommendation, but this volume was a "fun read." I enjoyed it! Don't get me wrong—Gilson's responses hit the skeptical objections at which he aimed time-and-again, including many of the major complaints lodged against Jesus' story. Tom didn't avoid head-on evaluations. But he did so in disarming ways that create a flowing narrative, revealing what made Jesus truly unique—doubtless the most influential life ever lived. Kudos!

Gary Habermas, Distinguished Research Professor, Liberty University

With so many books on Jesus, how do you say something fresh? My friend Tom Gilson has figured it out. *Too Good to be False* is an enjoyable read, well researched, and will challenge you to rethink some of your assumptions about Jesus.

Sean McDowell, Author, Speaker, Professor

A senior editor for *The Stream,* Tom Gilson produces articles that are well-researched and inspiring. It's no surprise that *Too Good to be False* has these same qualities. If you have never thought much about the impeccable character of Jesus or need a fresh reminder, you will be impacted by what Gilson shares in detail. As he writes, "The creator of our universe, Lord and King over all, unimaginably far beyond any of us in his holiness, greatness, and glory, loves us anyway, with a love far beyond our comprehension. He calls us his family; he calls us his friends." In response, may we fall on our knees in awe of Him.

James Robison, Founder and Publisher, *The Stream* (stream.org), Founder and President, LIFE Outreach International, Fort Worth, Texas

I was skeptical when I first glanced over *Too Good to be False.* My mind filled with objections that I knew my non-believing friends would give. But in a conversational, easy-to-read tone Tom Gilson demonstrates that the gospel narratives about Jesus simply could not be made up. To have "invented" Jesus would have required a genius that no human possesses. *Too Good to be False* meaningfully contributes to the world's apologetics library by affirming in a creative new way that Jesus was the most brilliant, loving, world-changing leader in history.

Jeff Myers, president, Summit Ministries

In *Too Good to be False,* Tom Gilson offers a fresh look at the argument for Christianity from the character of Jesus. Gilson's thesis is similar to C. S. Lewis's Liar, Lunatic, or Lord trilemma, but Gilson complements that argument in several ways. *Too Good to be False* offers insights into Jesus' less explicit claims for himself, based both upon what he does say and what he does not say. Several of these were new to me. For example, I appreciated the point that, when Jesus says that he came to fulfill the law rather than to destroy it, he is attributing high authority to himself. Would any ordinary Jewish teacher imply that he has the power either to destroy or to fulfill the Mosaic law? Gilson also points out the unprecedented nature of the Gospels' picture of Jesus as a man possessing vast, miraculous power but not using it to save himself from a shameful death. It is too easy to forget that this was hardly an ancient value, either Jewish or pagan, and it seems to have bewildered Jesus' own disciples. Our own love of a powerful, self-sacrificing "Christ figure" is conditioned by the fact that Christianity lies behind our culture. Skeptics, of course, deny that Jesus could do miracles, but Gilson asks how and why the evangelists came to put together these qualities and present the combination as an ideal if it were not true. He also illustrates that the Gospels' portrayal of Jesus' character is unified across a variety of stories, which is evidence of their historicity. *Too Good to be False* provides a welcome addition to the cumulative case for the truth of Christianity.

Lydia McGrew, Author of *Hidden in Plain View* and *The Mirror or the Mask*

If you've ever dreamed of being a lawyer, an investigative reporter, or maybe a detective, or if you love to ask questions, you will love this book. Reading it was as though I were sitting with Tom Gilson, meeting this amazing Jesus all over again. We marveled at his love and his goodness. Jesus' clever questions and brilliant responses, his leadership and humility all came alive. This book puts it all together: history, apologetics, a perfect character and unexpected humor. It offers insightful answers to hard questions, gives the skeptic some new ways to think about Jesus, and walks with me—and you—on a journey to let this Jesus live and love in and through us.

Judy Douglass, Author, Speaker, Encourager,
Cru Women's Resources, Office of the President

There's an old quip about great sermons that goes like this: "How long did it take to prepare that sermon?" The answer, "about 40 years." Tom writes from the perspective of a wise sage whose has written for many years, honing his thinking against the relentless barbs of unbelievers. *Too Good to be False* could only be written after that kind of legacy. But Tom doesn't write only as a tactician with carefully reasoned responses to tough questions. Rather, this book does something that seems rare for a book by a Christian apologist: It provokes worship. It moves us in the direction of not just right answers and right actions, but right affections, it provokes us to follow the leadership of the Holy Spirit to delight in the Lord Jesus himself! I'm grateful for this book and for what it will mean to those who will read it at my encouragement.

Gene Cornett, Teaching Elder, Bethany Place Baptist Church,
North Chesterfield, Virginia

Tom Gilson's book made me think about the Bible in fresh new ways—and helped me to answer certain nagging difficulties I've always had that made me read it *less* than I should. Enthusiastically recommended!

John Zmirak, author, senior editor at *The Stream*

My thinking and my approach to apologetics as a Christ-follower and a pastor have been reoriented through *Too Good to be False*. More compelling than good "arguments" are evidential reasons to believe in Jesus because of Jesus. I will be recommending this book to believers to strengthen their faith and embolden their witness *and* to spiritual inquirers to lead them *to* Jesus.

Brad Mitchell, Pastor, The River Church, Liberty Township, Ohio

Too Good to be False paints a refreshing portrait of Jesus' character as strong evidence that he couldn't have been "invented." Beyond this, I love the way Tom Gilson turns the tables on skeptics by exposing their presuppositions as the real drivers of their negative views. Tom also equips the reader to push back against the skeptics' trick of framing the issues to stack the deck for their positions. Good, solid rebuttals!

Glenn Pearson, Speaker, Author of *That's a Great Question:*
What to Say When Your Faith Is Challenged

In *Too Good to be False,* Tom Gilson examines the nature of Jesus and argues that the gospel descriptions of the Savior were too glorious, consistent, and unique to be the product of legendary embellishment. *Too Good to be False* describes the incredible character and appeal of Jesus of Nazareth, even as it makes a refreshing case for Christianity.

J. Warner Wallace, *Dateline* featured Cold-Case Detective, Senior Fellow
at the Colson Center for Christian Worldview, Adjunct Professor
of Apologetics at Talbot School of Theology (Biola University) and
author of *Cold-Case Christianity, God's Crime Scene* and *Forensic Faith.*

Tom Gilson is always a careful and patient apologist, taking the time to explore objections to the faith that others might dismiss. In this book, he argues persuasively that Jesus is a unique character in history. If you're open-minded skeptic, Gilson makes a strong case you probably haven't seen elsewhere. If you're already a believer, he reveals truths that have been right there in the gospels all along, but you probably haven't noticed. Do you want to know the truth about Jesus? Then this is the book for you.

Jay Richards, Best-selling Author, Speaker,
Research Assistant Professor, Catholic University of America

Tom Gilson takes a fresh, innovative approach in his stimulating *Too Good to be False.* Although oriented for the general reader—including skeptics—the "professionals" will get a lot out of it, too.

Craig A. Evans, John Bisagno Distinguished Professor
of Christian Origins, Houston Baptist University

Are you skeptical that anyone could present fresh insights about Jesus after two thousand years? Tom Gilson has done just that by highlighting what Jesus didn't say and do, which is almost as shocking as what Jesus did say and do. *Too Good to be False* not only gets you to say "wow!" about the most influential life in human history, but also helps you realize how feeble the arguments against the biblical Jesus are. I think you'll thoroughly enjoy this easy-to-read and hard-to-refute case. Extremely insightful!

Frank Turek, President, CrossExamined.org, speaker and
co-author of *I Don't Have Enough Faith to be an Atheist*

TOO GOOD TO BE FALSE

Too Good To Be False

How Jesus' Incomparable Character
Reveals His Reality

Tom Gilson

Too Good To Be False: How Jesus' Incomparable Character Reveals His Reality
© 2020 by DeWard Publishing Company, Ltd.
P.O. Box 290696, Tampa, FL 33687
www.deward.com

Cover design by nvoke design.

The preponderance of Bible quotations are taken from the The Holy Bible, English Standard Version®, copyright © 2001 by Crossway Bibles, a publishing ministry of Good News Publishers. Used by permission. All rights reserved. Any emphasis in Bible quotations is added.

Reasonable care has been taken to trace original sources for any excerpts and quotations appearing in this book and to document such information. For material not in the public domain, fair use standards and practices were followed. Should any attribution be found to be incorrect or incomplete, the publisher welcomes written documentation supporting correction for subsequent printing.

Printed in the United States of America.

ISBN: 978-1-947929-09-8

Contents

Foreword

This is a good book—a very good book; a *surprising* book, even. It's about the central person in The Good Book, the Bible. It's a book I wish I had written. It is as easy to read as it is contemplative to digest. While the readability can make it a fast read, don't do it. It isn't that kind of book. It is one that should be read slowly—not because of the depth of vocabulary but because of the depth of reflection it deserves. In Jesus' own words, the purpose of life is found in the knowledge of God (John 17.3). But that sort of knowledge is intended to be contemplative and relational, not merely informative.

As president of the campus apologetics ministry, Ratio Christi (Latin for 'The Reason of Christ'), and a former philosophy and comparative religions professor, I've done quite a bit of reflection on Christ as he may be considered among movement and thought leaders who have transformed the world. Jesus is unmatched.

The author of this book wants you to know that in a deeper way than you've known it before. A thoughtful Christian in both mind and heart, clearly, he has taken time to chew on the meat of the topic before writinxg *Too Good To Be False.* Tom Gilson served with me in leadership at Ratio Christi and for many, many more years before that served with Cru where conversations about Christ abounded in a place of diverse reflective viewpoints. His life experience in Scripture and in conversation with people are on display in this writing.

The subtitle accurately represents much of the content of the book. The author wastes no time capturing the imagination with story, humor, and illustration aiding his efforts to facilitate surprise in the reader for a fresh view of Jesus. It happened to me. It will happen to you. Not in many years of reading has my imagination been so allowed to wander and grasp new insights. Happily, it's a book that provides study questions at the end, a helpful tool for small groups to interact with and encounter beneficial discussion.

Although the book is written with Christians in mind, it will also have an appeal for skeptics. Given Gilson's background in ministry, considering a non-believing stance to the 'historical Jesus' and 'Christ of faith' is also in view. Let me give you three reasons why you should read this book.

First, to be enchanted (or re-enchanted) with the astonishing Jesus. Gilson draws your attention creatively to consider certain things that Jesus didn't say and didn't do, which serves to heighten our sense of wonder about him. While there are books talking about general leadership skills derived from Jesus, some of what we learn is not necessarily transferable but uniquely his. Jesus is unmatched especially when considering other famous movement leaders throughout literature. His incomparable love, his sheer brilliance and wit, and his alluring authority attracted the biggest movement the world has ever seen or would ever see. There are many surprising features of Jesus' life that we miss. This book helps illuminate some of them.

Second, to be confident rather than skeptical of who Jesus is by looking at why Jesus' character reveals that he's just too good to be false. He was no ordinary rabbi. His reputation is legendary in that it is well known, but it is no mere "legend" in the sense of being a story that's evolved well beyond fact. Skeptics scorn belief in his miracles as incredible deeds, but they miss Christ's most credible character, which substantiates and confirms his claims.

The heart cannot embrace what the mind cannot believe. But Gilson helps overcome the skeptical objections by considering the narrative of the Gospels. He doesn't simply point out facts but focuses on the personal character of Christ via conversation, story, and illustration to help put things into perspective and remove the skeptical barrier to make room for confidence.

Third, Jesus has become easy to take for granted, and we want to overcome this. Not only must we unlearn certain false assumptions, we need to help others unlearn them too. The reason people have come to lack wonder in Jesus is to some degree because of the consequences of the Enlightenment. Scientific progress has had the tendency to marginalize God and Christ. Also, there is the problem of pluralism (we have an aversion to any claims that Jesus is exclusive, in an age of inclusivity). But Jesus' story disallows any other option; he is far too special to be ignored, or to be one option among many. What do we do with a renewed and confident vision of Jesus? If God could have brought life without the death of Christ, he should have. But he didn't. This brings us back to faith. We must unlearn the societal notion of faith both as it relates to action and to knowledge, i.e., we underestimate the nature and role of faith in a knowledge tradition. Gilson helps us to understand what faith looks like and reminds us that it matters.

Enjoy the book. But love the brilliant and beautiful Christ.

Corey Miller, Ph.D.
President, Ratio Christi Campus Apologetics Alliance

Preface

I drafted this book before anyone had heard of the coronavirus, but I'm sending the final version to the publisher now just three days after the World Health Organization declared a global pandemic. It seems impossible to conclude this work now without recognizing the new reality in which it will be published.

There's little need to change the main content of the book. But this is a book about a story, a very good story and a true one, the story of Jesus. This virus is changing each of our own stories, inevitably and (I expect) for the rest of our lives. It could cut some of our stories short. Or so it seems from here, anyway—yet not really, for our stories don't end, not for a virus and not for any other reason. Our stories, each one of them, will continue forever, and how will they come out? That depends above all else on what we make of Jesus, and what we do with him. He is the center of this book; he must be at the center of our lives. My prayer is that those who know him already will find strong encouragement here to worship him more and follow him closer, and that those who have doubts about him will see good reasoning that will resolve their doubts.

It doesn't require a virus to make Jesus important in our lives. He always has been, for every person in every time and season. This pandemic only makes it plainer to see. It makes the hope we find in Jesus' unmatched life more apparent, too. It's because his story is good, incredibly good, even — too good to be false! — that our own stories may come out very good, too.

Too Good To Be False portrays a new view of Jesus' story that's actually an old one, too long forgotten. If you'd been alive in the 18th and 19th centuries, you'd have seen this view of Jesus quite frequently in the writings of the time, but for some reason it's been virtually lost since then. Today as I've sought to resurrect this high view of our Savior, I've relied greatly on these authors, to whom I must express a debt of real gratitude. You'll meet many of them in Chapter One. I trust I'll have a chance to say thanks to them in person someday.

In the present, though, I wish to give sincere thanks to the many friends, colleagues, and scholars without whom this book could never have been written. First, there were the readers who helped me refine this manuscript, correct errors, and develop its arguments. They're great thinkers and writers, every one of them: Lydia McGrew, John Zmirak, Brad Mitchell, Jonathan Witt, and Chip Tudor. Brad Mitchell and Chip Tudor were especially helpful to me in writing the Study Guide questions at the end of the book.

Thanks go to James Kushiner and *Touchstone Magazine* for publishing an early version of this argument, "The Gospel Truth of Jesus," in the May/June 2014 issue, and to evangelical textual scholar Dan Wallace, for giving me strong encouragement to expand and develop that early version. J. Ed Komoszewski was instrumental in that as well. My great friend Timothy McGrew has encouraged me in this project in more ways than I can name. Scott Cherry of Advance Ministries in Dearborn, Michigan gave similarly strong support. Nathan Ward, Jeff Crosby, and Daniel Horton sent me leads to helpful source material.

Lisa Ann Gosling and Crystal Crawford gave the book helpful mid-course edits, and Bethel McGrew did outstanding work in final editing. Nathan Ward, my publisher, has been a tremendous help in many ways, and deserves special thanks for his patience through multiple revisions of this book. My sincere thanks go to all these friends and helpers. Any remaining errors are of course my responsibility and not theirs.

Thanks also to leaders and staff at New Orleans Baptist Theological Seminary's *Defend* Conference, The River Church in Liberty Township, Ohio, and Auburn (Michigan) United Methodist Church for opening their doors to presentations on this material.

I'm thankful as well for the encouragement of friends associated with the Spiritual Readiness Project: Allen Shoemaker, Julie Reese, Lee Bollow, John Haddix, and Lou Schnorr, as well as Dan Libstorff and Mike McQuinn.

Above all, I am grateful beyond words to God for the gift of my incredibly patient, wise, giving, and beautiful wife, Sara, without whose patience, encouragement, and love I could have done none of this.

In view of the content of this book, there is only one person to whom I can properly dedicate it: our truly extraordinary Savior, leader, Lord, guide, and friend, Jesus Christ.

Tom Gilson
Centerville, Ohio
March 14, 2020

ONE

Seeing Jesus Through New Eyes

"We wish to see Jesus." —John 12.21

Jesus' story can still surprise you. Does that surprise you?

Yes, you know the story. You know how incomparably great Jesus was while here on earth; how he healed the sick, raised the dead, and died and rose again for us. That's Jesus, and he's real. It's the greatest story of the greatest life ever lived. Still, I'm sure I can say this with great confidence: Jesus is even greater than you knew, and he still has surprises for you.

He's certainly greater than I knew through my first 43 or so years of following him, as a U.S.-based missionary and eager student of his Word. It's not because I hadn't been looking closely at Jesus. I read the Gospels dozens of times during those years. I knew of his miracles; I'd studied his teaching. I'd pored over what the great New Testament scholars had to say. Over and over again I'd been persuaded that he was God in the flesh, he's the Second Person of the Trinity, he's our creator, sustainer, and savior.

If that was all anyone ever knew of Jesus, it would be more than plenty. Lately, though, looking at him from fresh new angles, I've been discovering he's greater than that. *Breathtakingly* greater. It's been there all along, but I'd missed it—never seen it in the Gospels, and never heard it in any teaching I'd sat under or any book I'd read. There still remain dozens of unexpected truths, points of greatness in Jesus' life, that virtually no one is seeing.

But how could that be? Many of us have read through the Gospels dozens of times. We've heard them preached even more often. How could there be anything left in them to surprise us? Haven't we had time enough already to see what the Bible has to say about Jesus?

We know what he said and did. We know what's in the story. Maybe we're too used to it, though. I'll admit that was true of me. I used to go to the Gospels not expecting much new there; maybe some new ways to apply their teachings to my life, but no new information about Jesus himself. But that changed when I started looking at him in a different light, studying what Jesus *didn't say*, and what he *didn't do.*

Yes, you read that right. This isn't your everyday Bible study method, I'll grant, so I'd better explain. It comes in two steps. It starts with seeing Jesus' difference compared with the best of the best, the greatest teachers and leaders the world has ever had to offer. I don't just mean the best in history; I'm even including the best of the best in *literature* and *legend*. As it turns out, Jesus' story—and specifically his *character*, the kind of person he was—stands out as unique. He's absolutely unique in real history, and he's just as one-of-a-kind when viewed next to all the myths, legends, and stories people have been telling since stories were first invented. But he's not just unique. He's *good*. Good beyond the goodness of any character any human has ever devised.

But that doesn't tell you what I mean about studying what Jesus *didn't* say and do. Some of that you'll need to discover as you read. Here's the short version for now: It's a process of looking at what great leaders and teachers typically say and do, and discovering how different Jesus was—and considering the difference that makes. His methods and teachings were, indeed, *very* different. More than *what* he did, though, there is the astonishing distinctiveness of *who* he was. It's not just his teachings and miracles that set him apart, but especially his character as an individual; a man like no other man.

Skeptics like to tell us his story is nothing special. There are lots of ancient, parallel "god stories," they say, and the plot points in his story are just like plot points in other ancient myths. Dig deep into all those supposed parallel stories, though, and you'll find that the parallels aren't what the skeptics say they are. But I'm not talking about plot points here anyway. I'm talking about the kind of person Jesus was—the life and character of the Gospels' central Person. For example:

- Jesus never used his extraordinary powers for his own benefit, but only for the sake of others. That's far more unusual, and far more loving, than most of us have grappled with.

- Jesus seldom quoted scripture as the source of authority for what he was teaching. More often than not, he was his own authority.

- He never called God "Our Father," except for one time when he taught the disciples *they* should say it.

- He never said he had faith in the Father, and nothing else in the Gospels says he did, either.

I can't tell you how it surprised me when that last fact hit me. After thinking it over, though, I came to see it made sense in very important ways. (I'll explain in Chapter Seven.)

There's more besides that, naturally. What I can't communicate so well in these short bullet points is how exhilarating these discoveries can be. It really is about seeing Jesus in an almost completely new light. Of course I'm not saying it leads to "new truths," for most "new truths" in Jesus studies are deceptive and false; they're the stuff that cults are born of. These discoveries are of the "how much more" variety instead: how much greater, more loving, *more clearly God*, our Savior is and was than I'd ever realized—even after 40-plus years of following him.

An Approach So Old, It's New Again

It was only after some work on this that I encountered something else that took me almost as much by surprise. These discoveries weren't so entirely new after all. They only *seemed* like it. While doing research for this book, I learned that other authors actually had written on Jesus' character this way, but it was a very long time ago. My findings weren't so new after all. Rather, they were so old, they'd become new all over again.

No other writer that I've been able to find has taken this approach to Jesus' character since Atticus G. Haygood in 1929. Haygood wasn't the first, though. Others that I located—with considerable help from several scholars, including Dr. Timothy McGrew, the world's leading expert on older Christian texts on reasons for belief—go back to the 1860s and earlier. Only one author since Haygood has even come close to touching on this topic: C. S. Lewis. (But of course! Who else?) You'll find a brief excerpt from that 1959 essay of his in Appendix A.[1]

Why the long silence, you ask? I have no way of knowing. It certainly isn't because the power of this perspective has weakened over time. The opposite is true, actually, especially where this approach addresses skeptics' theories that Jesus wasn't really who the

---

[1] Or you can read the entire essay online. Lewis, C.S., "Modern Theology and Biblical Criticism." In *Christian Reflections*, edited by Walter Hooper (Grand Rapids: W.B. Eerdmans Pub. Co. 1967). Available at http://orthodox-web.tripod.com/papers/fern_seed.html.

Gospels say he was; that his miracles and especially his resurrection are nothing more than "legend." Studying Jesus' character this way takes us straight to the opposite conclusion, the rock-solid conviction that Jesus must be real. He's too good to be false.

Skeptics Miss It, Too

Really? *Too good to be false?* Yes, really. Jesus' character is too great. His way of living in the world couldn't possibly be the stuff of legend—especially the way skeptics tend to think it was. There's good reason to doubt the "legend" theories, and to believe in Christ's reality instead, based in the greatness of his character alone.

Not that this is the only reason to distrust "legend" theories; far from it, actually. Responsible New Testament scholarship has uncovered all kinds of problems with skeptical legend conjectures.[2] There's something especially satisfying, though, in being able simply to look at the character of Jesus and draw an informed, responsible, and positive conclusion from that alone.

I expect skeptics will scoff at that. Many of them know his story just as well as Christians do, some of them even better. They'll tell you the Gospels are riddled with errors and all kinds of inventions dreamed up by the "faith community" that followed Jesus the rabbi. His miracles are impossible, they say. Take those away, and all that's left is another ordinary tale of another ordinary Jewish teacher. Bob Seidensticker, a prominent atheistic blogger, states it with admirable clarity:[3]

---

[2] Readers who want an updated overview of relevant New Testament scholarship might want to begin with Bock, Darrell L. and J. Ed Komoszewski, eds., *Jesus, Skepticism & the Problem of History: Criteria and Context in the Study of Christian Origins.* Grand Rapids: Zondervan Academic, 2019.

[3] Seidensticker, Bob. "Jesus: Just One More Dying and Rising Savior." *Cross Examined. Patheos,* April 15, 2012. https://www.patheos.com/blogs/crossexamined/2012/04/jesus-just-one-more-dying-and-rising-savior. Emphasis in the original.

Strip away any supernatural claims from the story of Alexander the Great, and you've still got cities throughout Asia named Alexandria and coins with Alexander's likeness. Strip away any supernatural claims from the Caesar Augustus story, and you're left with the Caesar Augustus from history. But strip away the supernatural claims from the Jesus story, and you're left with a fairly ordinary rabbi. The Jesus story is *nothing but* the supernatural elements.

Just a "fairly ordinary rabbi story," plus special effects; that's all Jesus is, for Seidensticker and most other atheists and skeptics. He's just a run-of-the-mill faith-founder, the kind that just about any religious community could have come up with. Sure, the story started with a real person, an actual Jewish rabbi named Jesus; most atheists and skeptics will grant you that. He preached; he gathered a group of followers; he died young; and that was it, or so they claim. It was over—except then his followers went on to embellish his story with a virgin birth, a resurrection, and dozens of other miracles in between—exactly the kinds of plot points that typically crop up in legends, they say.

But there's more to the story than these plot points. There's also Jesus' *character*, which is unique in ways that skeptics have completely missed. Look closely at him from that point of view, and you'll see this is no ordinary rabbi story. Neither is it an ordinary "god" story. Indeed, it's not an ordinary story *in any way at all.* You could even take the miracles out of it, and you'd still have a story absolutely unlike any other, for no other story has ever told of a person with *character* like Jesus'.

Worship-Enhancing and Faith-Building

Now, I know that not every Christian reader is all that concerned over skeptics' theories. That's okay. This book isn't primarily about rounding up skeptics' ideas and proving them wrong, anyway. It's mostly about gaining a fresh new vision of Jesus. My primary aim, for those who are already convinced he's worthy of their worship, is to show you even more reasons to fall on your knees in wonder before him. I've experienced that renewed sense of worship myself as I've studied this material, and I long to share it with other believers.

Meanwhile, though, there's also real value for us all in discovering new grounds for confidence in Christ. When faith comes under challenge, good reasons to believe can provide answers that satisfy the mind, besides encouraging the heart. They support our conviction that Jesus is worth following no matter what. And those who are wondering about Jesus, who think the skeptics just might have a valid point with their "legend" theories, can also be assured there's a strong case to be made here for Jesus' reality. My prayer is that this will even help persuade some of the skeptics that there's a better answer than the one they've thought was right all along.

Overview of the Book

So here's what to expect as you continue through *Too Good to Be False*. This chapter closes (after this overview) by reviewing the essential foundation: the basics of the life of Christ. Following that, the book is divided into three parts.

Part One is all about the surprisingly fresh truths I've been telling you about, plus more. Power and love meet in Jesus like they never have in any other person, or even any other character in literature. He assumes astonishing levels of authority. He displays a level of intellectual brilliance few believers have taken note of. He leads in ways that would never work if anyone else tried them, yet no one would call him a failed leader!

In Part One I also address in detail what I mentioned briefly above: The Gospels never say Jesus had faith. He almost never said, "Our Father," except once in Matthew 6, when he was instructing his disciples that they should say it. Far from mere trivia, these surprising truths strongly support Christianity's conviction that Jesus was God in the flesh.

Part One closes with a question inevitably raised by Jesus' greatness. You might expect that such a figure would be inaccessible, remote, far beyond human reach. If it were up to us, he would be. Instead, shockingly, he calls us his friends. (We'll come back to that in Part Three, too.)

Meanwhile, though, we can't forget that this is a story, although it can't be *just* a story. Jesus is too good to be false. In Part Two I look at some skeptics' alternate theories: how they think the "legend" of Jesus grew up in small communities scattered around the Mediterranean, each group with its own different needs and agendas, each of them altering the story, then passing the distorted version to the next community, so that by the time somebody somewhere finally wrote it down, the original facts of Jesus' life were either lost or hopelessly corrupted. Best of all, there's the psychological misfire that skeptics think got the whole chain of storytelling started in the first place. (It's all very entertaining, if nothing else.) The closer we look at it, though, and the more we compare it to Jesus as we saw him in Part One, the more we see their explanations just don't fit.

Part Two may seem to be pointed more toward those who don't follow Christ, but it matters for believers, too, for at least two reasons. First, surely there's someone in every believer's life who isn't totally confident in Christ. It might be your son or daughter, your grandchild, a classmate, or a colleague, who isn't sure it makes sense to believe. With this information, you can help them see how Jesus makes more sense as the truth than any kind of legend. Second, your own convictions will solidify even further as you see how skeptics try to tear down Jesus' story, and how far their attempt falls short.

Finally, Part Three answers the crucial question, once we have these new tools, *what do we do now?* Following Jesus wholeheartedly isn't just a matter of adding new truths to our store of knowledge. We've got some "false facts" to *unlearn*, too. For one, there's the typical pluralistic trope that it's wrong, rude, and arrogant to think there's only one way to God. It's downright immoral to say that Jesus is better than other religious founders, and especially to assert that he alone is the one way to God. Unfortunately for today's moral climate (but fortunately for the sake of our lives in Christ), his story won't allow any other answer. People can try to tell us every religion is a path to the truth. They can try to make Jesus one more entrée in the religion buffet. But we know Jesus well enough by now to know that he hasn't left us that option. He doesn't fit on any menu. Even secularists should be able to see the options are limited. There is no middle ground, allowing him to be one answer among many.

We have things to unlearn about *faith*, too. Even Christians get its meaning wrong. Is it really "belief without proof," as many say? Worse yet, is it "belief without even any evidence," as skeptics love to tell us? Far from it, as we'll see. The real thing is far more robust than that, and far more reasonable, too.

That concludes the main message of the book. An epilogue intended especially for pastors and other Christian leaders shifts the focus from Jesus himself to crucial, biblically-based ministry strategies for an age that's become too used to Jesus. It explains the biblical model I myself have sought to follow in writing this book.

Jesus' Life: The Basics

Before entering upon all that, though, I want to review the basics, the story of the life of Christ as we all know it.

It's familiar enough. It's told almost entirely in the four books, Matthew, Mark, Luke, and John, that open the New Testament.

The first three are called "Synoptic" gospels, from the Greek for "looking together." They're obviously similar in many ways, as if they're all "looking together" at Jesus, giving us one view from different angles. The fourth Gospel, John, portrays the same Jesus we see in the Synoptics, except it conveys much more openly the message that this Jesus is God among us. (Some people say that *only* John teaches Jesus' deity. We'll see about that in Chapter Seven.) Together, the Gospels weave a common, shared portrait of the greatest man who ever lived.

He was an extraordinary individual long before the start of his story among us, in view of the hundreds of Old Testament prophecies foretelling his life. And he was extraordinary from his beginning on earth. His virgin birth, with great signs and miracles surrounding it, signifies he was born of God. Christians since the beginning have always been clear on the belief that he was and is God in the flesh. Being in human form, however, he let go of some of the attributes of deity. As Philippians 2.7 puts it, he "emptied himself, by taking the form of a servant, being born in the likeness of men." He released hold of his *omnipresence*, most obviously: in his flesh, Jesus was no longer everywhere at one time. He emptied himself of at least some of his divine *knowledge* (see Matt. 24.36); how much, we cannot know. Yet he remained God in the flesh: one person with two natures, human and divine, a seeming paradox (yet not a contradiction) that ranks up there with the mystery of the Trinity.

He knew who he was, though. Even at age twelve, at the Temple in Jerusalem, he knew it well enough to explain to his earthly parents that Joseph wasn't his father, his Father in Heaven was. Otherwise, we know almost nothing of his life before age 30. He opened his ministry being baptized by John, with the voice of God proclaiming his approval from heaven. Then he spent forty days fasting and praying in the wilderness, after which he successfully resisted a series of temptations by Satan, exemplifying his entire life of consistent and complete righteousness. No one ever saw him disobey his Father in any way. He never fell short, not even in the hard instruction to love always.

He performed miracle after miracle, healing every sickness and disease, casting out demons, and demonstrating great power over nature. He preached the Kingdom of God: what that Kingdom is like, and what God requires of a person to be ready to enter it. He gave strong, wise, yet demanding ethical instructions; but the main key to life, he taught, lay in repentance and faith—faith in himself, "the way, the truth, and the life." He claimed to be the *only* way, for "no one comes to the Father but through me" (John 14.6).

He attracted followers, some seriously committed, others only curious about him. He made enemies, too, particularly among religious leaders whose power and prestige he threatened, whom he even labeled as hypocrites. They arranged with the ruling Roman authorities to have him tried on trumped-up charges, tortured, and killed on a Roman cross. A sympathizer named Joseph of Arimathea had him buried in his own rock-hewn tomb. On the third day after that, he was discovered alive again in glory, first by a small group of women followers, later by his entire band of disciples. For forty days he dwelt among them, showing up sometimes unexpectedly, interacting over meals and in long conversations. Then he was taken up into heaven before their eyes.

His followers, who had scattered in fear and discouragement at the time of his arrest, gained tremendous strength, courage, and faith through their experience with the risen Christ, and also, soon afterward, by God's arrival among them in the person of the Holy Spirit. They quickly began spreading a movement to worship and follow Jesus Christ—a movement that now numbers in the billions of people who consider him *actually to be God.*

From Familiar Overview to Fresh Vision

That's a quick and familiar overview. It's more than sufficient to be extraordinary to the believer, outrageous to the skeptic. For many of us, that's what there is to know about Jesus—that, plus his ethical teaching, which was world-changing at the time but seems rather familiar now. Even his death, resurrection, and ascension have become familiar. We know what Jesus did. We're used to it.

But what if we could see Jesus through fresh eyes? What if we discovered more to him than we've seen before? What if Bob Seidensticker (the atheist I quoted above) was wrong, such that even if we took the miracles away, Jesus' life would still be the most amazing story ever told? (Not that we *need* to discount the miracles, but that we'd look at Jesus that way strictly in response to his challenge.) What if his story's very uniqueness was strong evidence that atheists were wrong; that the story demonstrates its own truth, in ways the skeptics haven't even begun to imagine?

We can gain that fresh vision of Jesus. For Christians it will give deeper insight into who it is we worship when we declare him our Lord and our God, as Thomas did in John 20. For non-believers, it will give new reason to recognize the great and surprising truth of Jesus Christ.

So let's dive into these surprises now. We'll begin with unexpected truths about the uniqueness of Jesus' love.

PART ONE

Greater Than You Knew

TWO

Jesus' Astonishing Love

Is there one solitary defect, the very least, in this character that we find in the evangelists? Is there one weak spot, or suggestion of fault, or intimation of infirmity, or suspicion of failure, the slightest, to do and to be what was right for him to do and to be? —Atticus G. Haygood [1]

It was late in the first half. Notre Dame had the football, and they were moving it all too effectively. Things were bad for my team, Michigan State, and looking likely to get worse very quickly. I was there in the stadium with fellow students at MSU, none of us enjoying it one bit. That's when I said out loud, "This would be a great time for Notre Dame to fumble the ball." And they did—on the very next play. MSU got the football.

I made the most of it: "Hey, did you see that? I called it in advance!" But then it happened again in the second half—which was when it turned spooky. Notre Dame was advancing the ball again, things were still looking bleak, so I tried it again: "This would be another great time for them to turn it over to us again." And on the very next play, they fumbled it back to Michigan State.

I have to tell you, I felt relieved when I gave it a third try and it didn't work—even though we ended up losing the game.

---

[1] Atticus G. Haygood, *The Man of Galilee*, 1889 (Chillicothe, OH: DeWard Publishing, 2012), 5.

It hasn't worked since then, either. Of course, I knew it wouldn't; it hadn't actually "worked" the first two times, either. Those two fumble calls were nothing but lucky coincidences. But that didn't stop my friends from saying, "Whoa, Tom! I don't know if you can be trusted with that kind of power!"

It got me thinking, riding along a wild and imaginary train of thought that I couldn't help following. *What if I really could do that? What would it be like?* I could turn the sporting world upside down. I'd make a killing on bets. With power like that, I could control players' careers and gamblers' fortunes—at least until some bookie figured it out, and sent someone after me.

I'd like to think I'd have handled it the right way, Jesus' way: that I'd have had the wisdom to know it was unethical to interfere that way, and the strength of will never to use the power again. But this I know for certain: it would have driven me mad, just knowing that it was there, that it was something I *could* do if I wanted. Or "needed." Because the days inevitably come when you need some extra cash. The car breaks down. Or your family is relocating, and you're a few thousand bucks short on the down payment for the house you really want. You call a bookie, place a bet, cause the fumbles necessary to make sure your team wins big, and all your problems are solved.

No one would ever guess a thing. Not even your family would need to know (other than maybe wondering where the windfall came from). Too bad for the losing teams, though, especially the players who got blamed for the fumbles you caused. It might even rob them of an NFL career.

Sure, it's nothing but fantasy. Still, it makes a point, because my friends were right. There isn't a person among us who could be trusted with that kind of power. Abraham Lincoln put it well: "Nearly all men can handle adversity, but if you want to test a man's character, give him power." Lord Acton's saying still rings true long after he wrote it: "Power tends to corrupt, and absolute power corrupts absolutely. Great men are almost always bad men."

No Good Powerful Person But Jesus

Yet there *was* a man who walked the earth, carrying infinitely more power than that. Football games? Child's play! Jesus changed the weather with a word. He made a boy's lunch big enough to feed thousands. He raised people from the dead.

Did he misuse that power? Never. Did it drive him mad? The furthest thing from it. Jesus did the right thing every time. And here we come very quickly to one of the most surprising facts in Jesus' life, the first great point in our study of *what Jesus didn't do:* he never let his extraordinary powers control him. He never even used them for his own benefit. It was always for others. "For even the Son of Man came not to be served but to serve," he said in Mark 10.45, "and to give his life a ransom for many."

Jesus is the lone, striking exception to an otherwise universal human reality: Character tends to crumble when it obtains too much power. I couldn't even imagine staying sane with the power control football fumbles. Indeed, from corrupt popes to rotten politicians, from greedy tycoons to marauding military men, history is filled with stories of powerful people going bad.

Literature is, too. Where do you know of any great stories of extremely powerful, truly self-sacrificial and giving people?[2] Not that it's hard to invent such a story. It's just hard to make it *interesting.* I can prove it in one second: "Alvin got a new superpower when he turned twenty-five. He was so powerful, he could do whatever he wanted. He got up every morning and used his power

---

[2] Other than those directly modeled after Jesus, that is, as Superman was from the beginning; and also, by extension, every other superhero modeled after Superman since then. Plus, we'll see later how far Jesus outshines even Superman.

only to help others. It never even occurred to him to use them to do anything for himself. Everyone loved him. The end." That's not exactly what you'd call a memorable character!

There's been a growing trend in superhero movies for heroes to feel conflicted, troubled over the right and the wrong they find inside themselves. We know why writers do that, of course: it's to make the characters that much more interesting. Shakespeare understood this. That's why he brought us the sadly flawed Hamlet, Lady Macbeth, and Richard III. Goethe gave us Faust. Tolkien gave us Saruman the White, who went mad with his power. Even Gandalf knew that the power of the Ring would be his ruin, if he were to exercise it. Not one of the greatest writers of all time has been able to compose a compelling story of an all-good, all-powerful person.

Jesus' Unmatched Goodness

Yet in the midst of them all, there stands the great exception: Jesus Christ, the one man out of all history and literature who has great power but consistently uses it for others. Indeed, Dietrich Bonhoeffer rightly called him "the man for others." Though he often grew weary, still Jesus gave of himself—because he cared *for others*. He taught—*for others*. He traveled, always *for others*. He died for no reason except *his love for others*.

> And Jesus went throughout all the cities and villages, teaching in their synagogues and proclaiming the gospel of the kingdom and healing every disease and every affliction. When he saw the crowds, he had compassion for them, because they were harassed and helpless, like sheep without a shepherd. Then he said to his disciples, "The harvest is plentiful, but the laborers are few; therefore pray earnestly to the Lord of the harvest to send out laborers into his harvest" (Matt. 9.35–38).

This only begins to plumb the depths of his love. He gave his life for us, willingly and freely. This, too, was unique, more so than we commonly recognize. We've all said at one time or another, "I don't want to die!" Some of us have come so near death we've prayed, "Not now, God! Don't let me die!" But aren't we still just negotiating with God over the time and the method? We all know we're destined to die, if Jesus doesn't return first.

Jesus was different. There was no negotiating with death for him. He entered it purposely and intentionally. He alone had the option never to die at all. Death is the penalty we pay for sin, but he had no sin. He didn't have to suffer the injustice of the trial and sentencing, he didn't have to suffer the beating, and he didn't have to die on the cross. Yet he chose it all—for us.

In fact, there's one way in which his sacrifice was *even more voluntary than that.*

The Only Man Who Ever Gave His Consent to be Born

You've heard of crazy lawsuits, right? This one might top them all. Early in 2019 I read in the news about an Indian man, Raphael Samuel, who filed suit against his parents for bringing him into the world without his consent.[3] "Life was imposed on me," he complained. "I want to make it a legal right for a child to sue a parent. ... Ideally the parents should not have the child. But if they do have the child, they must compensate the child." I get the sense he'd have let go of the complaint if only he'd signed a waiver before he was born. Informed consent, you know. Then his parents would have been off the hook.

That's silly, of course. No one gives their consent to be born; no one but Jesus, that is. It isn't just that he didn't have to die for our sins. *He didn't even have to be born.* He chose it freely, in will-

---

[3] "The Man Who Gave His Consent to Be Born." *The Stream*, February 19, 2019. https://stream.org/man-gave-consent-to-be-born/.

ing obedience to the Father. Unlike every other human who's ever lived, he had that option, and he said, "Yes, I'll do it." He freely gave up the rights and prerogatives of his eternal godhood and condescended to being born like any other human baby. And he did none of it for himself. Only for us.

Everything Jesus did by his extraordinary powers, he did for others. He could have saved himself from the cross, but he remained there for our salvation. He had the power to make food, even feeding 5,000 at one time, but do you recall how he answered the devil at his point of extreme hunger, following forty days of fasting? Satan took one of his best-ever shots at him:

> And the tempter came and said to him, "If you are the Son of God, command these stones to become loaves of bread." But he answered, "It is written, 'Man shall not live by bread alone, but by every word that comes from the mouth of God'" (Matt. 4.3–4).

He had the power, but he didn't use it for himself. He never did.[4]

Imagine Yourself That Giving?

I try to imagine myself being that good, but I can't. Not even close. Earlier I imagined having the power to control football games. Now I'll bring it slightly back down to earth. (*Very* slightly.) This time I'm imagining coming into loads of money. Not long ago the Powerball payout rose to nearly $1 billion. Someone had to win it, or at least a good share of it. What if it had been me? (Not that I play the lottery, but this is all imagination, right?) Suppose I had also determined I would be the most giving, self-sacrificial billionaire in all history. I'd only want to do good with all that cash. I'd commit to giving it all away: to missions, to feeding the poor, to

---

[4] Some commentators suggest an exception in Matthew 17.24–27, where Jesus has Peter go catch a fish, find a coin in it, and pay the temple tax for the two of them. To me, it looks more likely that Jesus is teaching Peter an object lesson than that he's providing for a need of his own.

stopping sex trafficking, and other great, giving things. That would be amazingly noble on my part, right?

Here's the thing, though. Apart from being terribly impressed with myself for doing so much good—an attitude you never see in Jesus!—I'm sure I wouldn't go all the way with it. Would you? Wouldn't you get the brakes fixed, at least? Or the roof, or the furnace? You'd take your family out for a nice dinner, wouldn't you, or maybe even a week at a resort? And who could fault you for it? What's a few thousand bucks or two for yourself, out of the hundreds of millions you'd be giving away? As for me, I'd probably upgrade my computer, too—"so I could write more books for the Lord." Very giving of me, don't you think?

Jesus was more giving than that. He didn't win the Powerball, but then, he didn't need to. He had far, far more power than a billion dollars could command, yet he never took himself out for a nice dinner on that power. He didn't take any resort vacations. When he used his power, he used it for others. All of it. As William Paley wrote,[5]

> Neither as represented by his followers, nor as attacked by his enemies, is he [Jesus] charged with any personal vice. ... This faultlessness is more peculiar than we are apt to imagine. Some stain pollutes the morals or the morality of almost every other teacher, and of every other lawgiver.

Indeed, "some stain" pollutes us all, and all the more as we gain more power. But not Jesus.

If you or I tried to write the stories of ourselves that way, it would be unbelievable, an obvious fabrication. We can only be who we are, and every one of us falls far short of Jesus' standard of perfect love.

---

[5] Paley, William, *A View of the Evidences of Christianity: in Three Parts,* (New York: Robert Carter Brothers, 1859), 138.

This is no light matter. There is something awesome—almost terrifying, even—in Jesus' goodness: knowing that he lived a life of perfect love, and that we fall so short of that love he commanded us to live by. Herein lies almost unapproachable majesty. We could excuse our lack of love with "What did you expect? *No one* is perfect." Except Jesus *was* perfect. He showed it could be done. He even showed how to do it.

The uniqueness of Jesus' love will play a key role in the case I make in Part Two: that he's too good not to be true. But there are still more discoveries to be made before we get there.

THREE

Jesus' Surpassing Brilliance

Can we seriously imagine that Jesus could be Lord if he were not smart? ...
How could he be what we take him to be in all other respects and not be
the best-informed and most intelligent person of all, the smartest person
who ever lived? —*Dallas Willard*[1]

I was shopping for snacks at a newsstand at the Orange County airport in California. A man approached me, maybe 30 or 40
years old, hair balding, dressed in vest and beads—or as I call it,
"California creative" style. He pointed toward the rack where the
magazine covers were hidden behind plain brown paper. Only
their titles were visible: *Playboy, Hustler,* and *Penthouse.* "You really
ought to buy one of those," he said.

That caught me off guard, I'll tell you. I didn't know anything
better to say, so I simply answered, "No, thanks."

He wouldn't give up , though: "Oh, you don't know what you're
missing!"

"No, thank you," I repeated, "I'm a happily married man." I left
as fast as I could. And ever since then I've kicked myself for not
saying this instead:

"No, you're the one who doesn't know what he's missing! You're
pushing fake relationships with fake paper-thin women. I have a real

---

[1] Willard, Dallas, *The Divine Conspiracy: Rediscovering Our Hidden Life in God*
(San Francisco: HarperOne, 1998), 94.

relationship with a real woman, someone who's committed the whole rest of her life to me, just as I have to her. She knows me and she loves me, as completely as any woman could love. We share the intimacy that comes from trust; trust you could never even imagine. I wouldn't trade that for anything. That's what you're missing!"

I've told this story many times since then while teaching the value of solid, committed, trusting marriage relationships, so I guess I can say I've gotten some good out of it. Still, though, I wish I'd said that to him when I had the chance. We've all had that sort of experience, haven't we? We've all missed giving the right answer when we could have. Worse yet, we've all said the wrong thing at the wrong time.

Everyone except Jesus. You think I was caught off guard there at the airport? I think of what Jesus ran into every day: repeatedly accosted by enemies trying to trap him; entreated by sick people asking for miracles; approached by pretenders who acted interested but weren't really ready to follow him. Some he debated, some he healed, many he challenged. Sometimes, surprisingly, he left the conversation dangling. In one case (John 11, when Lazarus was sick) he waited four days before answering. In another instance—quite a shocking one—he scolded Peter, "Get behind me, Satan!" In another, he wept for the lost city of Jerusalem.

Never once, though, in all these varied and difficult encounters, did he ever walk away saying, "Well, I missed it. Hope I do better next time."

My favorite story along these lines appears in Luke 20.1–8 (with parallel passages in Matt. 21.23–27 and Mark 11.27–33).

> One day, as Jesus was teaching the people in the temple and preaching the gospel, the chief priests and the scribes with the elders came up and said to him, "Tell us by what authority you do these things, or who it is that gave you this authority." He an-

swered them, "I also will ask you a question. Now tell me, was the baptism of John from heaven or from man?" And they discussed it with one another, saying, "If we say, 'From heaven,' he will say, 'Why did you not believe him?' But if we say, 'From man,' all the people will stone us to death, for they are convinced that John was a prophet." So they answered that they did not know where it came from. And Jesus said to them, "Neither will I tell you by what authority I do these things."

We'll return to this passage later to examine the Jews' mistaken belief that *they* had authority to demand that *he* explain *his* authority. For now, though, see how effectively Jesus responded: he got them into a political squabble among themselves, thus demonstrating for all to see that they were power seekers, not truth seekers. They had asked him to reveal his source of authority; he got them to reveal their sorry character instead.

What kind of man was Jesus? Brilliant. Here's one more thing he never did: He never walked away saying, "You, know, I could have said that better." He got it right every single time.

"The Best and Smartest Man Who Ever Lived"

It was Dallas Willard who first woke me up to Jesus' brilliance, in his book *The Divine Conspiracy*. Jesus was, said Willard, quite simply "the best informed and most intelligent person of all, the smartest person who ever lived." He had to be, for how else could we entrust our lives to him? He was (and is) "the master of intellect." He "knows the truth about our lives and our universe."[2]

We see it from the very beginning of his teaching. I'll never forget my friend Adam's first sermon after seminary. That's not his real name; he wouldn't much like hearing what I thought of that sermon. It was awful. He rambled. He made factual errors. His

---

[2] Willard, Dallas, *The Divine Conspiracy: Rediscovering Our Hidden Life in God* (San Francisco: HarperOne, 1998), 94.

style was—*yawn*—sleepy. My wife and I were both thankful when it was over. Now, though, we're thankful the church gave him more opportunities. Adam grew over time, and with added experience and some coaching, he's become quite an outstanding pastor and preacher. Moral: You have to give people grace. No one gets it right on their first try.

No one but Jesus. By Matthew's timeline, his first sermon was the Sermon on the Mount. I join many others in considering it the finest sermon ever preached; a *perfect* sermon, even. It was a sermon for the ages—literally: we're still talking about it 2,000 years later. Again, Jesus got it right the first time, as he did every time, in every way.

Jesus' intelligence was belied by the simplicity of his methods and language. But the substance behind them was as solid as could be. Consider his parables in particular. How much simpler could any teaching be than that? But how perfect his parables were in that simplicity! Every teacher knows it's easy to make simple subjects look complicated, and hard to make complicated ones look simple. Jesus did it unerringly, every time. As William Paley wrote,[3]

> The parables of the New Testament are, many of them, such as would have done honour to any book in the world: I do not mean in style and diction, but in the choice of the subjects, in the structure of the narratives, in the aptness, propriety, and force of the circumstances woven into them; and in some, as that of the Good Samaritan, the Prodigal Son, the Pharisee and the Publican, in an union of pathos and simplicity, which in the best productions of human genius is the fruit only of a much exercised and well cultivated judgment. The Lord's Prayer, for a succession of solemn thoughts, for fixing the attention upon a few great points, for suitableness to every condition, for sufficiency, for conciseness

---

[3] Paley, William, *A View of the Evidences of Christianity in Three Parts* (New York: Robert Carter Brothers, 1859): 133.

without obscurity, for the weight and real importance of its peti-
tions, is without an equal or a rival.

The "aptness, propriety, and force of the circumstances woven
into them"—three terms that speak to the parables' power and fit-
ness to do what Jesus intended. Think of some of the most famous
of them. The Prodigal Son is such a short story; so is the Good
Samaritan: so simple, yet how much is contained in them! Their
simplicity is a mark of their brilliance.

Brilliant in His Understanding

Jesus also had a genius for understanding people and their spiritual needs. Every individual is different, and he had a way of understanding those differences. We can see his wisdom clearly in the
way he spoke with different groups or types of people.

First, there were the crowds. His message in the Sermon on
the Mount (Matt. 5 through 7) was clear as the mountain air—on
one level. "Love your enemies," he said. That's pretty straightforward—and yet how much effort have theologians and pastors put
into explaining it! The same goes for the Beatitudes, the Lord's
Prayer, and in fact the whole rest of the Sermon. He taught his
parables with no intention of explaining their full meaning to the
crowds (see Matt. 13.11–15). With the crowds, in other words, he
was willing to leave a lot unanswered. I'm convinced it's because he
wasn't there to satisfy their theological curiosity. Rather, he wanted
to draw them in to following him as Savior and Lord. He had to
awaken that thirst in them. He had no desire to satisfy them with
mere information, when he'd come to give them himself.

Then there were his adversaries. Study his debates, especially
in the middle chapters of John, and you'll see he wasn't primarily
interested in answering the religious leaders' questions, but more
in shaking them loose of their pride and hypocrisy. He knew that

what they needed most wasn't the information he could have supplied; rather, they needed to see themselves for who they were, so they might repent and follow him.

As for the disciples, they may have been a rotten bunch at times, arguing over who was the greatest, and with Peter even denying him. But they'd committed to following him, which is what he sought. So when they asked questions of him, he didn't hold back as he did with the crowds or the Pharisees. He opened up and gave them "the secrets of the kingdom of heaven" (Matt. 13.11).

Never Plays It the Way We Would

Everything Jesus did, he did brilliantly. Yet in almost every case, he did it in ways unlike the rest of us would. Or as my friend Dan Loughran says, "Jesus never plays it the way we would have." Dan is right. Jesus was master of the unexpected answer. Greg Gilbert said it this way:

> Once people began to challenge him and ask him questions, Jesus proved to be a masterful chess player. He simply refused to get caught in verbal or intellectual traps, and in fact always managed to turn the heat back on the one who posed the challenge in the first place. And even then, he did it in a way that would not only win the argument, but also spiritually challenge everyone listening.[4]

Horace Bushnell wrote,[5] "Never was there a teacher that so uniformly baffled every expectation of his followers, never one that was followed so persistently."

A Jewish leader came to him by night (John 3) and buttered him up, saying, "We know you must be from God, otherwise you couldn't do the things you do." Jesus ignored the schmooze and gave him an answer Nicodemus must have considered totally off

---

[4] Gilbert, Greg, *Who Is Jesus?* (Wheaton, IL: Crossway, 2015), 30.

[5] Please see my clarifying note on Bushnell in the Resource Guide at the back of this book.

the wall (or he would have, had they used that phrase back then). "You must be born again," said Jesus. Now, where did *that* come from? From his wisdom. Nicodemus was a "teacher of Israel," and probably quite self-satisfied in his learning and knowledge. He needed to learn what it feels like to be confused. Then maybe he'd be ready to listen and learn from Jesus.

Another man told Jesus he wanted to follow him, and Jesus answered, "Foxes have holes, birds have nests, but the Son of Man has nowhere to lay his head" (Matt. 8.20). Again: where did that come from? From Jesus' wisdom. This man apparently didn't know the real cost of following Jesus, and needed to give it proper consideration before diving into something he wasn't ready for.

The religious leaders tried to trap him with a question about taxes to Caesar, and he replied, "Render to Caesar what is Caesar's, and to God what is God's" (Matt. 22.21). Where did that come from? From his wisdom, so much greater than ours. He maintained full allegiance to the Father, while ducking the political trap they'd laid for him. Later, though, when the time was right, he walked willingly into their trap, accepting the trial, the beating, the crucifixion—and turned that trap into the greatest of victories.

Who would play it the way Jesus did? Only a true genius. In all his encounters, he knew. He knew exactly what each person needed, and how best to deliver it. Who else has ever been so skillful and understanding? His interactions were brilliant on that account.

Never Deliberates

And how did Jesus acquire all this knowledge? There are lots of theories out there, many of them laughable. The BBC did a documentary in 2018 suggesting that Jesus spent his late boyhood and early adulthood as a Buddhist monk in India and Tibet.[6] Besides

---

[6] "BBC Documentary: Jesus Was A Buddhist Monk Named Issa Who Spent

lacking all evidence, somehow this theory overlooks the fact that his life and teachings have much to do with the Law, the Prophets, and the Kingdom of God, and absolutely nothing to do with Buddhism. You'd think that would seem important, wouldn't you?

Yet we do have a mystery here. It's not just that we don't know what he did up to age thirty. We know what he *didn't* do after he entered public ministry. As Atticus G. Haygood notes, "Jesus never investigates." He just knows.[7] Haygood goes on,

> He never doubts his knowledge or questions for one instant the grounds of it. We have no fit word for his method; intuition is perhaps as good as any. His thinking is not a process; it is like seeing, not learning, the truth; seeing not the outside of things as men see them, but the inside of them as God sees them.

We never see him deliberating, either, as Anthony Esolen has pointed out. We don't see him pondering; never see him needing time to weigh the facts. Yes, he spent the night in prayer before choosing the Twelve, which could be one exception to that observation—except we don't know whether he was deciding whom to choose, or praying for them by names he already had in mind, or simply praying for the ministry he would soon launch with them.

We do know that in public dispute he was consistently, instantly ready with an answer. Horace Bushnell says it this way:[8]

> He does not speculate about God, as a school professor, drawing out conclusions by a practice on words, and deeming that the way of proof; he does not build up a frame of evidence from below, by

16 Years In India & Tibet." *Humans Are Free*, March 2018. http://humansare-free.com/2018/03/bbc-documentary-jesus-was-buddhist-monk.html.

[7] Haygood, Atticus G., *The Man of Galilee*, 1889 (Chillicothe, OH: DeWard Publishing, 2012), 34.

[8] H. Bushnell, *The Character of Jesus, Forbidding His Possible Classification with Men* (New York: The Chautauqua Press, 1888), Kindle ed., 2010, Kindle loc. 474

some constructive process, such as the philosophers delight in; but he simply speaks of God and spiritual things as one who has come out from Him, to tell us what he knows.

He just knows.

Jesus' Miracles

We think of Jesus' miracles as acts of great power, which is certainly true, but we should also think of them as acts of great knowledge. In John 2, for example, Jesus spoke, the water obeyed, and it turned into wine. Seems straightforward enough, right? Except water doesn't know how to do that. It can't "obey" on its own. So how did it happen?

Some of us might have the wrong idea, supposing (unconsciously, I'm sure) that Jesus was tapping into "mysterious unseen forces," almost like an early sort of Harry Potter. The reality was nothing like that. Yes, the "force" was unseen, but we know who it was: God himself. That means either it was Jesus making wine from water on his own power as Second Person of the Trinity, or else it was one of the other Persons. If Jesus, then he had to know his ethyl from his methyl alcohol—one of which is drinkable, the other quite poisonous—not to mention all the other complex compounds in fine wine. And that was on the easier end of the miracles he performed. When he calmed the sea, multiplied the loaves, and healed the people, he had to know in detail how the world works, from the minutest subatomic features to the grandest system of them all, the human body and soul.

Yet he made it all look so simple. He spoke a word, and people rose from death. He prayed and broke bread, and somehow suddenly there was more of it—a *huge* amount more. He commanded the wind and waves, and they obeyed. He did it simply, easily, and humbly. There were no equations on the blackboard to prove he knew his physics and chemistry. Just frequent acts of absolutely, completely well-informed power.

Now, if instead the work was done by the Father or by the Holy Spirit, Jesus wouldn't have needed all that knowledge of physics, chemistry, biology, meteorology and the rest on hand while in his human state. Instead he would have needed intimate, unerring knowledge of the Father's will in every circumstance. That would be no less intellectually amazing; in fact, it would be far more so. We have chemists who know the difference between ethanol and methanol, and could even tell you the molecular formulations of the esters that give wines their distinct flavors. But intimate knowledge of the Father's will? That's still *way* beyond any human's reach.

So no matter how we look at his miracles, Jesus was displaying a mind like the world had never seen before, and never since, either.[9]

Jesus' Poise, Equanimity, Balance

Jesus handled every interaction—every challenge or opportunity—with complete and unmatched poise. Watch him as he goes from one encounter to the next, and see how serenely he stays on top of it all. He never goes off balance, not even in his anger. There's just one place the Gospels explicitly tell us he was angry, and it wasn't at the cleansing of the temple, as most think. It was in Mark 3.1–5.

> Again he entered the synagogue, and a man was there with a withered hand. And they watched Jesus, to see whether he would heal him on the Sabbath, so that they might accuse him. And he said to the man with the withered hand, "Come here." And he said to them, "Is it lawful on the Sabbath to do good or to do harm, to save life or to kill?" But they were silent. And he looked

---

[9] Skeptics are undoubtedly saying at this point, "No, in fact, Jesus did it exactly the same way Harry Potter did: *fictionally!* It's *all* fiction." I have an answer for them, but I'm saving it for Part Two.

around at them with anger, grieved at their hardness of heart, and said to the man, "Stretch out your hand." He stretched it out, and his hand was restored.

The leaders of the synagogue had two men standing before them: Jesus, and a man with a withered hand. Their attention was focused on Jesus: Could they catch him in the grave sin of doing work on the Sabbath? As for the man with the withered hand, he was nothing more than a prop, a tool, a convenient opportunity for them to get at Jesus. They were using him.

No wonder Jesus was angry. Yet his anger was matched by his grief. I know of no better way to keep anger contained and focused where it belongs. It was the same grief that poured out of him while weeping over Jerusalem: the grief he felt for men and women who would not open their hardened hearts to the love and grace of God the Father:

> And when he drew near and saw the city, he wept over it, saying, "Would that you, even you, had known on this day the things that make for peace! But now they are hidden from your eyes. For the days will come upon you, when your enemies will set up a barricade around you and surround you and hem you in on every side and tear you down to the ground, you and your children within you. And they will not leave one stone upon another in you, because you did not know the time of your visitation" (Luke 19.41–44).

Time after time the religious leaders tested Jesus. Time after time they used innocent, even disabled bystanders to trip him up. Time after time, even his own disciples tested his patience. In Matthew 16.21–23, it was Peter's attempt to tell Jesus, "This shall never happen to you;" later, on the night of Jesus' trial, it was Peter's outright denial. And how much patience Jesus displayed, even with the Pharisees, scribes, and lawyers, when he pronounced his woes upon them (Matt. 23; Luke 11.37–52)! These "whitewashed tombs, full of dead men's bones" were deserving of judgment right then; but he hadn't come for that. Not this time, anyway.

Yet it was more than mere emotional poise that he displayed. His character was extraordinarily balanced in every way. Every strength has its weakness, they say. The most merciful people are often the ones least able to speak a strong word of needed correction, while the best admonishers are often the last people you want around to help heal a wounded soul. The best communicators are often the worst managers, and vice versa. We don't see that in Jesus, though. He has all of the virtues, with none of their corresponding vices.

As Joseph Canavan wrote in 1929,[10] "Our virtues easily run to excess, and we starve one quality in developing another;" but Jesus "harmonizes all the virtues. ... He alone ... found the secret of combining contrary qualities in such nice proportions that they mingle in him to form a flawless character."

Charles Edward Jefferson had said much the same in 1908:[11] "We are all overdeveloped on one side of our nature and underdeveloped on the other. It seems to be well-nigh impossible to keep our faculties in even balance. If we are strong in certain characteristics, we are well-nigh certain to be weak in the opposite characteristics." But Jesus, said Jefferson, was

> imaginative, full of poetry and music ... but he was never flighty. He was practical, hard-headed, matter of fact, but he was never prosaic, never dull. ... He was courageous but never reckless, prudent but never a coward, unique but not eccentric, sympathetic but never sentimental. ... He was religious, the most profoundly

---

[10] Joseph E. Canavan, "The Problem of Jesus Christ." *Studies: An Irish Quarterly Review* 18, no. 69 (1929):52–54

[11] C.E. Jefferson, C. E. "The Poise of Jesus." Excerpt from *The Character of Jesus*. Thomas Y. Crowell & Co, 1908. https://godtreks.com/2013/12/07/the-poise-of-jesus.

religious man that ever turned his face toward God, but never once did he slip into superstition. …not one of the enemies of Jesus was able by unfairness or falsehood or hatred to push Jesus into a hasty word or an unrighteous mood. … Jesus was so firmly poised that under the pressure of the most venomous vituperation that has ever been hurled against a man, he stood erect, unmoved, and immovable. His poise was divine.

Brilliant in His Emotional Intelligence

The light of Jesus' brilliance shines well beyond his intellect and into his character and emotional balance. If Jesus is impressive for never getting an answer wrong, he is even more so for never getting his *way of answering* wrong. With the weak he is tender, but to the strong he brings the force of his mind and his authority. His opponents may try to trap him, yet you can almost see him smiling as he turns the tables on them. It's a sad smile, though, for he was, as Isaiah said, "a man of sorrows, and acquainted with grief"—the grief of Mark 3.1–5; the sadness of one who knows how desperately others are damaging themselves, and carrying others with them.

Nowhere is this more apparent than in his trial, torture, and crucifixion. No man has ever submitted so completely to the harsh will of others, while yet retaining all control himself. In his passion he displays perfectly the paradox of power expressed in humility, explainable only by his purpose, to die for our sins. Thus at his arrest, when one of those with him strikes a servant with his sword, Jesus rebukes him, saying, "Do you think that I cannot appeal to my Father, and he will at once send me more than twelve legions of angels? But how then should the Scriptures be fulfilled, that it must be so?" (Matt. 26.53–54)

Pilate, bewildered at Jesus' silence during his trial, demands of him, "You will not speak to me? Do you not know that I have authority to release you and authority to crucify you?" Jesus replies calmly, "You would have no authority over me at all unless it had been given you from above. Therefore he who delivered me over to you has the greater sin" (John 19.10–11).

On the cross he cries out the agony of the human life he was giving up, yet in his divine love and grace he forgives his executioners (Luke 23.34).[12] And when a thief on a cross next to him begs for mercy, he turns his attention to that man's needs rather than his own: "Truly, I say to you, today you will be with me in paradise" (Luke 23.43).

He arranges for his mother's care from the cross: "When Jesus saw his mother and the disciple whom he loved standing nearby, he said to his mother, 'Woman, behold, your son!' Then he said to the disciple, 'Behold, your mother!' And from that hour the disciple took her to his own home" John 19.26–27. Is it any wonder a centurion standing there says, "Truly this man was the Son of God!" (Mark 15.39)?

In every test, even the greatest imaginable, Jesus maintained his composure. More than that, he kept on caring. He showed the greatest compassion when he should have most been the object of pity. He loved, even through the immensity of his pain.

No man's life has ever compared to Jesus. Neither has any man's death. Neither has any man's resurrection! But we'll return to that in Part Three.

---

[12] While there is some room to question whether this prayer was originally in Luke's Gospel, solid scholarship still backs its inclusion. See Jongkind, Dirk. "'Father Forgive Them'—The Variant in Luke 23:34a." *Evangelical Textual Criticism*, March 23, 2018. http://evangelicaltextualcriticism.blogspot.com/2018/03/father-forgive-them-variant-in-luke.html, and Burk, Denny. "Did Jesus Pray, 'Father, Forgive Them'?" Denny Burk: *A Commentary on Theology, Politics, and Culture,* January 24, 2011. http://www.dennyburk.com/did-jesus-pray-"father-forgive-them"/.

FOUR

Jesus' Authority

He teaches the world as one who had learned nothing from it, and is under
no obligation to it. —Philip Schaff[1]

Mistakes can be embarrassing, but confession is good for the soul,
so I'll go ahead and admit it: There's a line in Scripture I got wrong
for years. "And when Jesus finished these sayings, the crowds were
astonished at his teaching, for he was teaching them as one who
had authority, and not as their scribes" (Matt. 7.28–29). I thought
Jesus' crowd-astonishing authority meant he was supremely confident in front of large groups. He was thoroughly prepared; he
never stuttered; he never said "um" or "er." And he must have had
a *really deep, thundering voice.* He would have won Toastmaster of
the Year, every year, hands down.

Of course Jesus was both competent and confident, but I no
longer think that has much to do with the "authority" that astonished the crowds. Something else was going on instead. To
understand it, let's try to get into the crowds' mindset, only from
a more current point of view. Think of yourself on the job. You'd
never write a report without showing your sources: where you

[1] Philip Schaff, *Person of Christ: the Perfection of His Humanity Viewed as a Proof of His Divinity,* Kindle ed. (Hannibal, MO: Granted Ministries Press, 2013), Kindle loc. 483.

got your data, which experts would support your conclusion, and what the literature has to say.

Now, imagine a new fellow comes along, telling you, your bosses, and even their bosses they've got everything wrong, and he's come to set them straight. When you ask him to cite the research, relate his own experience, and name the experts who would back up his opinion, he says, "No, really, there's no need for any of that. It's true because I say it is." You'd have him dragged him out of there in half a second.

But that's exactly the way Jesus taught, isn't it? "It's true because I say it is." He never cited sources. If he'd been writing rather than speaking, he'd have used no footnotes. Or if he had, every one of them would read, "Source: Jesus of Nazareth." Himself. No one else. *Now* do you see why that would astonish his listeners?

Footnotes

Ah, yes, footnotes. Readers expect them, want them, *need* them. They serve as proof that authors know what they're talking about. They're also the roadmap to fact-checking and further study. My footnotes in this book do *not* read, "Source: Me."

The story is told (I have no idea whether it's true) of two British gentlemen arguing over dinner about some fact of nature (or maybe it was geography or history). One of them said, "I'll tell you what, old chap. Let's look it up in *Britannica*." The other gentleman agreed, went and found it on his bookshelf, read the entry, then admitted, "Well, I guess you were right after all." To which the first man replied, "Yes, I rather thought that was what I'd written there." Very few of us have that kind of authority. Even that scholar's word wasn't good enough, though; he still needed the editors of *Britannica* backing him up.

The scribes in Jesus' day called on their authorities, too. The Jewish *Talmud*, formed across the space of several hundred years starting around the time of Jesus' life, gives a good example of the rabbis' use of authority at that time. Though it varies from section to section, the first few pages are sufficient to show us what it was like. It begins, "What time should one recite *Shema* in the evenings? According to Rabbi Eliezer, from the time that *Kohanim* enter to partake of *teruma,* until the end of the first [night-] watch; the [majority of] Sages say, until midnight; Rabban Gamaliel says, Until dawn." There alone we have two named sources, not to mention "the majority of the Sages." In the next few pages the *Talmud* cites at least twenty different sources as authorities.

There's nothing wrong with that. We want our teaching to be given with competent authority behind it. Jesus met that expectation, but in a totally different way: His authority was his own, and that was good enough. He never mentioned the rabbis, except in passing: "You have heard that it was said." Then he explained how they'd gotten things wrong. Elsewhere, he used Scripture in various dialogues, especially when tested by adversaries, as in the question of marriage in Matthew 19.1–4. He quoted Scripture when the devil tempted him, and in Luke 4.18–19, he spoke of himself as the fulfillment of prophecy. But when he gave his Sermon on the Mount, it was entirely on his own authority. No sources needed; just his word.

Dallas Willard wrote, "Scribes, expert scholars, teach by citing others. But Jesus was, in effect, saying, 'Just watch me and see that what I say is true.'"[2] Or as Willard also said just prior to that, *"He himself was the evidence for the truth of his announcement about the availability of God's kingdom"* (italics in the original).

He Pulled It Off, Too

No wonder the crowds were astonished. Only Jesus could teach that way. You and I could never get anywhere skimping on our sources.

---

[2] Dallas Willard, *The Divine Conspiracy: Rediscovering Our Hidden Life in God* (San Francisco: HarperOne, 1998), 20.

I got hammered over that in grad school. My sin? I'd written a paper on servant leadership—which has received a lot of attention in leadership studies over the past several decades—and I cited Jesus as the original source of the servant leadership idea. The grad assistant grading my paper didn't think the Bible met the approved standard for peer-reviewed scientific sources. I appealed his decision; I lost. *Oh, well.* There are standards, and we must live with them.

The crowds in Jesus' day knew the standards, too. Their scribes would never skimp on citations, yet Jesus passed over them almost completely. And he did it in the hardest sort of message of all: introducing new, innovative moral teachings. This is one more on the list of Jesus' accomplishments that should surprise us more than it does.

He Got It Right

How can we even begin to describe the majesty of his moral teaching? Of course it wasn't all completely new; there were strong foreshadowings in the Prophets, for example. Jesus was quoting Isaiah 61.1–2 when he told his fellow Nazarenes,

> The Spirit of the Lord is upon me,
>> because he has anointed me
>> to proclaim good news to the poor.
> He has sent me to proclaim liberty to the captives
>> and recovering of sight to the blind,
>> to set at liberty those who are oppressed,
> to proclaim the year of the Lord's favor (Luke 4.18–19)

That was a familiar Old Testament quotation, but he wasn't quoting anyone when he sat down and said, "Today this Scripture has been fulfilled in your hearing" (vv. 20–21). *Fulfilled,* he said! By himself! On his own authority! Who says such a thing? Who could possibly have the *right* to say it? Only Jesus.

Let's return to the Sermon on the Mount. It's full of unexpected teachings. We hardly blink when we come to the last of the Beatitudes. We should, though, because there's quite a surprise to be found here, especially for certain scholars and skeptics who think the only signs of Jesus' deity are in the Gospel of John:

> Blessed are you when others revile you and persecute you and utter all kinds of evil against you falsely on my account. Rejoice and be glad, for your reward is great in heaven, for so they persecuted the prophets who were before you (Matt. 5.11–12).

One surprise is that persecution carries blessing with it. We're rather used to that, though. The real shocker is in the three words, "on my account." Take note of the parallelism there: The prophets before them were persecuted on account of God, while today we may be persecuted on account of Jesus—and the two amount to the same thing. To persecute the messenger of Jesus is *morally equal* to persecuting the Old Testament prophets of God.

Calmly, almost invisibly—how often have we overlooked it?— Jesus was making a claim of equality to God.

Speaking of the prophets, you've undoubtedly noticed they were in the habit of saying, "Thus says the Lord." They spoke that phrase more than 440 times between them. How often did Jesus say it? Exactly zero. He did cite the Father as support for his authority, as we'll see in a moment, but he never put it in quite the same way as the prophets. They always spoke *for God*, never as if it were their own words. Jesus, in contrast, spoke his own truth, with himself as the authoritative source behind it. Now, observe this carefully: he wasn't speaking *for God* as the prophets did, yet he spoke with the authority *of God*. The only way to make sense of that is to recognize he was speaking *as God*. I doubt the crowds on that mountain caught the full implications of what he was doing, but they certainly sensed something out of the ordinary in his teaching.

The Sermon on the Mount is filled with such surprises, if we'll only take time to recognize them. Here's another one. Suppose next time your church had a guest speaker he stood up, gave a few opening words of encouragement, and then assured the congregation most solemnly, "Do not think I have come here to abolish the Bible. I'm not here to abolish it, but to fulfill it." You'd have him quickly escorted from the platform, and not just because he said he was the Scriptures' fulfillment. It's outrageous even to say, "You needn't worry that I've come to abolish the Scriptures." It'd be like a man with a pickaxe telling his friends, "Don't worry, I'm not planning to level all the mountains."

But this is precisely what Jesus said in Matthew 5.17. Apparently there existed some real danger that people might think he'd come to abolish The Law and the Prophets. Who would even hint at having that kind of authority?

Jesus never lets up relying on his own position as his authority from which to teach. "You have heard," said Jesus,

'Do not commit murder,' …

'Do not commit adultery,'…

'Here's how to do a divorce,' …

'Here's how you make oaths,' …

'Here's how you ensure justice,' …

and,

'Here's who you're supposed to love.'"

Of course, he was right to say they'd heard all these things. And Jesus corrects all of them, simply on his word. Who was he to say the old rules were wrong? (We know the answer, but the crowds there didn't.) Granted, two of those instructions he let stand, except he added to them, saying it's not enough to say no to committing murder; we must say no even to calling anyone a fool. It's not enough to avoid committing adultery, we must avoid even thinking lustful thoughts. He speaks as one who has the right to add to the law, and to overrule what had been "said" about divorce and oath-making. Jesus "teaches the world as one who had learned nothing from it," said Philip Schaff, "and is under no obligation to it."[3] I don't recommend you try that at home.

This incredible sermon has altered the course of history. And Jesus taught it without citing a single source as his authority, not even Scripture. Nothing but his own life. That's why the crowds were astonished—and we should be, too.

Lord of the Sabbath

Of course there are other examples of authority in Jesus' teaching. Notice the matter-of-fact way he speaks of himself as greater than the Temple in Matthew 12.6–8: "I tell you, something greater than the temple is here. And if you had known what this means, 'I desire mercy, and not sacrifice,' you would not have condemned the guiltless. For the Son of Man is lord of the Sabbath" (Matt. 12.6–8). He's also claiming authority over the Sabbath. How does he prove it? He doesn't. He just moves on to the next moment in his ministry.

In Luke 4, Jesus encounters a man "who had the spirit of an unclean demon." He rebukes the demon: "Be silent and come out of him!" When the demon left the man, the people "were all amazed and said to one another, 'What is this word? For with authority and power he commands the unclean spirits, and they come out!'" (Luke 21.43–46).

Three Witnesses to His Authority

The crowds ate it up. The religious leaders? Not so much. Their displeasure with him came to a head in the middle chapters of

---

[3] Philip Schaff, *Person of Christ: the Perfection of His Humanity Viewed as a Proof of His Divinity*, Kindle ed. (Hannibal, MO: Granted Ministries Press, 2013), Kindle loc. 483.

John—the one place where Jesus actually defended his authority before his adversaries.

Let's set the stage. In John 7 Jesus had come to Jerusalem secretly, revealing himself later (verse 37) by crying out loudly in the temple, "If anyone thirsts, let him come to me and drink. Whoever believes in me, as the Scripture has said, 'Out of his heart will flow rivers of living water.'" Now, that's bold. Not just the loud voice, but especially the words. It was just one of many striking claims he made in the presence of the religious establishment.

Later, when we reach the end of that chapter, we find the people divided over him. The chief priests and Pharisees were of one mind, though: Jesus was undermining their authority. They didn't believe in Jesus, so why were the people—including the Jews' own officers!—being "deceived" (verses 45 to 49)? These leaders were used to the crowds following them—or following "Moses," as they claimed in John 9.28—but the people were veering off to follow "this man," whom "we do not know where he came from" (John 9.29). If they hadn't stamped him with their seal of approval, the crowds shouldn't have approved of him, either!

All that is found in chapter 7 (with a bit borrowed from John 9). Next comes a brief interlude with the woman taken in adultery (8.1–11). Immediately after that, Jesus forced the authority issue again, telling the people (8.12), "I am the light of the world. He who follows me will not walk in darkness, but will have the light of life." The Pharisees noted—quite astutely, I might add—his lack of footnotes (as I've put it). "You are bearing testimony about yourself," they said in verse 13. "Your testimony is not true."

Was Jesus threatened by this? Not in the least. In fact, he escalated his claims. "Even if I do bear witness about myself, my testimony is true."[4] In other words, "I don't need any other witness.

---

[4] Yes, in John 5.31 he had said, "If I alone bear testimony about myself, my testimony is not true." But he was speaking in another context there, and empha-

I speak on my own authority." Try *that* in a court of law someday. Or in a paper you submit at school. Or while answering your boss, or even a customer. No, on second thought, don't try it; not unless you're the number one, top acknowledged expert in your field. Experts have the right to speak on their own authority, within their disciplines. The religious leaders didn't think much of Jesus acting like the expert in theirs.

Jesus could have stopped and left it there, but he didn't. Knowing the Scriptures say one witness is insufficient, he went on in verse 18 to name another: "I am the one who bears witness about myself, and the Father who sent me bears witness about me." That made two, so now it was, "I say so, and God says so."

And I wonder if we ought to be reading this with a sense of humor. He'd told the Jews they were wrong. They'd said, "Oh, yeah? Who says so?" He answered, "*I* said so." "Oh, yeah? You and who else?" "Me and the Father, that's who else!" I doubt he played it that way, though. I might have, but Jesus had perfect humility. I don't suggest you try that approach in your next workplace dispute, at any rate. Or family squabble. Or even your next religious debate.

Back to the story: The Pharisees didn't get it. They'd heard nasty rumors: Joseph wasn't Jesus' father, so who was? They pressed him on it, probably hoping to embarrass him: "Where is your father?" They couldn't know that one of his own disciples would ask him that same question in the Upper Room:

> Philip said to him, "Lord, show us the Father, and it is enough for us." Jesus said to him, "Have I been with you so long, and you still do not know me, Philip? Whoever has seen me has seen the Father. How can you say, 'Show us the Father'? Do you not believe that I am in the Father and the Father is in me? The words that I say to you I do not speak on my own authority, but the Father who

---

sizing the testimony he had also received from John. Here he is emphasizing his right to speak on his own authority.

dwells in me does his works. Believe me that I am in the Father and the Father is in me, or else believe on account of the works themselves" (John 14.8–11).

Where was Jesus' Father when the Pharisees were asking him that? In a unique and very real sense, he was right there with them. "He who has seen me has seen the Father." Thus, Jesus had the scripturally required second witness.

Not only that, but earlier (John 5.29–47) he had spoken of a third witness, meanwhile dropping in a further unexpected bombshell: "You search the Scriptures because you think that in them you have eternal life; and it is they that bear witness about me" (John 5.39). Later he added along the same lines, "Moses wrote of me" (John 5.46).

It's impossible for us to grasp just how outlandish that would have seemed to them. Imagine the next presidential candidate saying, "Thomas Jefferson mentioned me—me, personally, I mean—in the Declaration of Independence." That would be about the same kind of claim Jesus made.

Anyway, by this point Jesus had three witnesses: Himself, his Father, and the Scriptures. And then there were the miracles. Jesus pointed at them too in his disputes with the Jews (John 10.37–38). "If I am not doing the works of my Father, then do not believe me; but if I do them, even though you do not believe me, believe the works, that you may know and understand that the Father is in me and I am in the Father."

It wasn't the first time he'd said something along these lines. The earlier account is in Mark 2.1–12. Four men had brought him a paralytic to be healed. Instead, Jesus told him, "My son, your sins are forgiven." Scribes sitting there knew that no man had authority to forgive sins—not sins committed against God, anyway. We can forgive people the wrongs they do *us*, but no one but God can forgive sins committed against *him*. Jesus knew they were thinking that. He took up the challenge, and made it a challenge upon them instead:

> Why do you question these things in your hearts? Which is easier, to say to the paralytic, 'Your sins are forgiven,' or to say, 'Rise, take up your bed and walk'? But that you may know that the Son of Man has authority on earth to forgive sins"—he said to the paralytic—"I say to you, rise, pick up your bed, and go home."

And the man was healed.

Still the Pharisees were hard to satisfy. They wanted their footnotes. They wanted Jesus citing the same authorities they used. Better yet, they wanted to show Jesus up as a fake; to demonstrate that he had no right to speak at all. They certainly didn't want him running around usurping their position among the people; especially since he was telling the crowds that they, the Pharisees, weren't good enough. (That bit of divine chutzpah shows up in the Sermon on the Mount, in Matthew 5.20; it's one more reason the crowds recognized a claim of authority in his message.)

So they and their cronies came and tested him. Remember the story from Luke 20 we looked at earlier—the one where Jesus bested them by asking them about John the Baptist's authority? Let's recall again how that exchange began:

> One day, as Jesus was teaching the people in the temple and preaching the gospel, the chief priests and the scribes with the elders came up and said to him, "Tell us by what authority you do these things, or who it is that gave you this authority" (Luke 20.1–2).

They thought *they* had authority to demand Jesus explain *his* authority. Wrong. After he'd set them debating amongst themselves, he gives his answer (verse 8): "Neither will I tell you by what authority I do these things." Debate over. They had nothing on him. Jesus didn't need their permission. He didn't need footnotes. He was his own authority.

He Made It Work

And he made it work. Thousands of years later, his moral authority still guides the world. If ever there was a sign that Jesus was God, this is it. Yes, of course, there are other signs, many of them; but this one certainly needs adding to the list. Just think what it would take to introduce a challenging, seemingly impossible new moral standard like "Love your enemies." You'd certainly need to practice what you're teaching. Since that's really quite impossible for most of us, you might want to try plan B: "Here's this great new moral teaching. It's urgent that you follow it. Or at least try. Do the best you can. That's all I'm trying to do myself, even though everyone can see I'm not up to the task. What did you expect, anyway? I'm only human." But Jesus lived up to his teaching.

Our generation has succeeded in all kinds of innovation: communications, travel, medicine, data management, business theory, you name it. Moral innovation, though? That's a different story. Even where people have tried introducing new moralities—granting approval to homosexuality, for example—they've sought to build their case on old moral principles like love and equality. They haven't succeeded, in my considered view, but that's a story for another day.[5] My point for now is this: real moral innovations don't come along every day; not even every century! How could they? No one even lives up to the old standards, much less any new ones they might introduce.

No one but Jesus, that is. He said, "Love your enemies," and he lived it, all the way to the Cross. He did the same in all his teachings. History itself agrees he got his ethical principles

---

[5] See my 2015 Kregel Publications book, *Critical Conversations: A Christian Parents' Guide to Discussing Homosexuality With Teens.*

right—not only in his words but in his walk. And he did it on his own. That's extraordinary.

Authority Assumed, Authority Demonstrated

Jesus demonstrated his authority by his miracles; he argued for it with the Pharisees; he proved it in practice. That's familiar enough; but again, seeing it in light of what Jesus *didn't do*, and what he *didn't say*, draws the picture even clearer. He didn't use "footnotes." He never said, "Thus saith the Lord." He never backed down from his claims of authority, and he never failed to practice what he preached. No one else has even come close.

FIVE

Jesus' Paradoxical Leadership

*Other leaders and reformers have relied on others, whose opinions or ad-
vice would give balance to their views. Jesus had none; He needed none.*
—R. E. Speer[1]

There's authority and then there's leadership. We all know what
happens when you have one without the other. I've had bosses
whose position gave them all the authority they could ask for, but
couldn't lead a rope by pulling on it. I've also seen people with great
leadership skills, frustrated by lack of authority. Maybe you've felt
that way yourself at some point in your career.

Jesus wasn't lacking in authority, but neither was he that other
unpleasant character, the one who can't lead. (I trust you'll pardon
the understatement there.) Anyone who founds a movement that
grows and grows across thousands of years, reaching billions of
people, has done something very, very right as a leader.

This is familiar enough territory, isn't it? But what if I told you
there was something in Jesus' leadership that makes it even more
surprisingly great? There is; and again, it starts with something we
hardly ever notice. Or if we do, we never discuss it, possibly because it feels wrong to bring it up. It's completely unexpected and

---

[1] Speer, R. E. *Studies of The Man Christ Jesus: Studies of what Christ was, His
Character, Personality traits, His Spirit, Himself.* Kindle loc. 1587.

paradoxical; so much so, the best way to introduce it might be to imagine certain character traits of Jesus being practiced in today's leadership world. I'll do that by means of this highly imaginary memo sent from one corporate vice president to another.

MEMO

FROM: Cheryl Sanders, VP Operations

TO: Rob West, VP Human Resources

SUBJECT: Midwest Manager Hiring Candidate

Rob, I've got a new candidate, Jack Benson, to lead our Midwest Group. I wanted to run his profile by you before deciding on him. Jack comes highly recommended, and he has some real positives going for him, but I have my doubts. Tell me what you'd think of hiring someone like this:

- I can't find anyone who'll say they've ever seen him learn from experience, especially from any of his own mistakes.
- No one says he's ever even *admitted* to making a mistake.
- His leadership skills haven't improved one bit since he started out.
- I've checked his bio, and I can't find a single sign of any character growth in him. Not even a trace of it.
- Rarely will he give a straight answer when you ask him a question.
- If you've got an opinion and it's different than his, well, you're just wrong.
- It's "do it my way" with him—his way or the highway. No exceptions.
- He won't even be friends with anyone who won't do what he "commands." Yes, he actually does use that word.

So, what do you think, boss? Should we hire him?

How would you like working for a boss like that? If I were the VP who got that memo, I'd shoot one right back, short and to the point: *"Are you kidding? He'd have to be God in the flesh to get anywhere leading that way!"* Because truly only God, here in the flesh, could have a profile like that and still persuade people to follow him. Yet that is exactly what Jesus did.

There's no denying his leadership effectiveness. People followed him gladly when he was alive. That's a good start. Billions of people 2,000 years later still follow him, which is a great deal *more* than a good start. So the lesson of this memo obviously isn't that Jesus failed as a leader; rather, it tells us he succeeded in a manner that no other leader could. Later in this chapter we'll explore what it was that allowed him such amazing success, despite traits that organizational theorists today would describe as huge leadership deficits. We'll see they aren't deficits at all, in his case; but more than that, we'll discover even more reasons to be amazed at his greatness.

But first, let's tease out the character traits from that memo a little further.

Mistakes? Me? Never!

First, Jesus didn't learn from mistakes. He didn't *admit* to any mistakes. And he didn't *improve* following any mistakes. There's only one way a leader could make that work: *Never make a mistake.* Have you met anyone who can do that? Sure, some leaders may be oblivious to their errors, but that's not what we're talking about here. Try to imagine having a boss who was just completely unaware of anything wrong—ever—in his life, his decisions, his leadership style. Can you think of anyone you'd want to work for less than that?

I served for several years as an HR director in a major mission agency. I would never recommend anyone for leadership if he or she couldn't readily answer the question, "Tell me about a time you've failed, and what you learned from it." Jesus couldn't have answered that. He didn't learn from his personal failures; he didn't grow through his mistakes; he didn't have any to learn or grow from. Contrast that with two of the greatest leaders of recent centuries, Abraham Lincoln and Winston Churchill, both of whom failed often and spectacularly. Both of them lost multiple elections before being voted in as president or prime minister. Both learned through their multiple failures. Those experiences steeled them to lead with the character they needed through the wars they each had to deal with.

I'd hate to tell you how often and how badly I've fallen short as a leader. In my first real leadership position I annoyed literally everyone, the whole team, by expectations they didn't understand, and the tone of voice I sometimes used. It wasn't they who were wrong, it was I. So I learned: I softened my expectations, and I put someone else in charge of the one recurring situation where my tone bothered people the most. Still, some members of my team never thought I'd learned enough. They were right, naturally; I've made even bigger leadership mistakes since then. But I've learned from them. I'm a better leader and better person for it.

No Improvement

Here's the strange thing about Jesus, though: He never got any better. That wasn't just in his intelligence, as we saw in Chapter Three; he never improved at *anything* in his ministry. Imagine having that on your own performance review, year after year: "He never improves." Not much of a vote of confidence, is it?

Luke 2.40 and 2.52 do say he grew in wisdom, but there's no detail there. I can easily imagine him learning from error in Joseph's shop: "Now, Jesus, do you see the lesson you've just learned?

Measure twice, cut once!" The Bible doesn't say he never made a mistake, only that he never made any *moral, ethical, spiritual,* or even *relational* mistakes. He never committed sin, in other words, and he never missed the truth when he spoke. He might have learned to be a better craftsman as he was growing up, but that's not the kind of growth we're talking about here.

Now, the Bible does say he "learned obedience through what he suffered" (Heb. 5.8). But did he learn to obey *better?* No. He clearly demonstrated complete obedience right from the beginning when he faced Satan's temptations, which took place long before the greater part of "what he suffered." So what this passage actually means is that he learned the experience of obedience in the face of suffering. Or you could say he learned *what it's like* to obey while suffering. He learned what we go through, in a way that never could have been possible had he not come in the flesh. Thus, he became a High Priest who can sympathize with our weaknesses (Heb. 4.15).

From the first moments of his adult ministry, there's no sign of anything less than fully developed and fully competent leadership, character, integrity, wisdom, knowledge, and power. And he was only thirty years old! Which of us could say that of ourselves at that age? Have you ever met anyone who got it right the first time, the way Jesus did, *every* time? Again, the only way to make that work in practice is by starting out perfect.

Few Straight Answers

Back to the memo: Leaders give straight answers, right? Suppose you've got a question for your boss, and you approach him, saying, "Boss, we need to know if we've got budget for the new office build-out." And he answers, "Truly, truly I say to you, the resources you seek, you will find where you least expect them."

(Or something like that. You wouldn't believe how hard it is to write an example that sounds like Jesus.)

Jesus actually made a point of not giving straight answers. I've counted, and when Jesus had the opportunity to answer a question—other than requests for healing, that is—he gave a straight answer only once out of every five times. Often he'd answer with a question of his own. Sometimes he would leave the person more confused than they were before. Remember poor, bewildered Nicodemus in John 3, asking, "What? Do you mean a man has to enter back into his mother's womb?" There was no straight answer from Jesus there, at least not at first.

But we know that Jesus had good reason for not giving direct answers. He wasn't concerned about production the way most leaders are. He wanted souls worthy of his Kingdom. No one but Jesus could lead that way.

Who Asked Your Opinion?

Jesus never asked for others' opinions, either. The closest he came was when he asked questions such as, "Who do others say that I am? Who do you say that I am?" But he wasn't fishing for new knowledge in these instances, he was using those questions to teach. Even when he asked Phillip in John 6.5, "Where shall we find enough bread to feed this crowd?" he already knew what his own answer would be. His disciples had nothing to teach him, everything to learn from him. That's why Jesus' interest in his followers' opinions could be boiled down to:

- Do you understand what I'm telling you? and

- Are you going to do it?

And also, just as far out of the ordinary:

- Do you love me? (John 21.15–17)

Remember when Peter offered a contrary opinion on Jesus' crucifixion? Jesus shot back, "Get behind me, Satan!" You call that a sound leadership style? Only for Jesus. Sometimes he asked people what they wanted, and often he'd supply it for them, especially in his healing ministry. But there was never any doubt that it was his decision, and his alone. If this isn't making you wonder, "Then why did *anyone* follow him?" it really should be.

But let's not rush too quickly to answers. We need to grasp the full depth of the question that needs answering: why did people follow an honest-to-goodness know-it-all like Jesus? Yet they did. If he told them to let down the nets on the other side of the boat, they did what he said; they let down their nets on the other side. The fact that they had years more experience fishing meant nothing. With Jesus you did what you were told. Period.

It really was "his way or the highway," or as he said in John 15.15, "You are my friends if you do what I command you." (We'll return to that in Chapter Eight.) There's no wiggle room there. You say you want to follow him? "Leave the dead to bury their own dead," he said. No negotiating, even on a family matter like that. No one could dispute him. Hardly anyone dared talk back at him, and if they did, it always came out the worse for them. He was more than willing to show people the door for not doing things his way. Or even for not dressing the way they should, as he put it in the parable of the wedding feast (Matt. 22.1–14): "Then the king said to the attendants, 'Bind him hand and foot and cast him into the outer darkness. In that place there will be weeping and gnashing of teeth.'"

A leadership style like that never should have worked. It did, though. His disciples followed him all the way to their own deaths. Why? How could Jesus lead so effectively, while breaking just about every leadership rule in the books?

Why Jesus—and Jesus Alone—Could Break the Leadership Rules

Jesus didn't need to learn from his mistakes, because he never made any. He never needed advice because he already knew. He acted like he knew it all, because he actually did. That's a great start, yet there must be more to it than just that. Being right all the time isn't all it takes to attract willing, lifelong followers. Think of the brilliant surgeon who's got a half-dozen surgical residents learning from him every year, and who never makes a mistake in the operating room. He's always right in that environment, so they'll follow him that far. Outside the OR, though? They might not want anything to do with him.

In sharp contrast to that, Jesus' followers—the true ones—followed him everywhere. He must have had more going for him than just being right. And of course, he did: His followers knew he loved them, that they could trust him, and that he really did have the authority to lead the way he did.

Jesus' Love and Humility

I spoke of the great, giving quality of Jesus' love in Chapter Two, but let's follow that story a few steps further. Considering all he had going against him in terms of standard leadership traits, why did people follow him anyway? Above all else, it must have been his overwhelming, supernatural love. He served (Mark 10.45) in humility, caring, and radical other-centeredness. That's the kind of man who attracts followers. The disciples died for Jesus because Jesus died for the disciples.

It was his humility, too; but not ordinary, self-effacing, human humility. His was *self-emptying*, as only God could empty himself. Philippians 2.5–8 tells it beautifully:

> Have this mind among yourselves, which is yours in Christ Jesus, who, though he was in the form of God, did not count

equality with God a thing to be grasped, but emptied himself, by taking the form of a servant, being born in the likeness of men. And being found in human form, he humbled himself by becoming obedient to the point of death, even death on a cross" (Phil. 2.5–8).

This was the highest expression of love, and also Jesus' highest glory, for as the passage continues,

Therefore God has highly exalted him and bestowed on him the name that is above every name, so that at the name of Jesus every knee should bow, in heaven and on earth and under the earth, and every tongue confess that Jesus Christ is Lord, to the glory of God the Father" (Phil 2.9–11).

Jesus' Trustworthiness

And he was trustworthy. He set a perfectly consistent example of high integrity. He displayed it in his love and obedience toward his Father, in his Kingdom-focused mission, and in his constant emphasis on truth. Therefore, when he said, "Follow me," people could have full assurance that he, too, was obeying God. They knew God's Kingdom was a desirable destination. And they could believe he was speaking truth at all times.

People don't willingly follow leaders they don't trust, but they knew they could confidently follow Jesus.

Real Authority, Expressed in Humility

Jesus had the authority to lead. He could take charge because he really was in charge. He was no usurper, no pretender; he really was God in the flesh. He was the long-awaited Messiah, the King whose kingdom was already real, though its final manifestation remains yet to be revealed. Still it's astonishing how gentle he was in view of that.

Behold, my servant whom I have chosen,
>my beloved with whom my soul is well pleased.
I will put my Spirit upon him,
>and he will proclaim justice to the Gentiles.
He will not quarrel or cry aloud,
>nor will anyone hear his voice in the streets;
a bruised reed he will not break,
>and a smoldering wick he will not quench,
until he brings justice to victory;
>and in his name the Gentiles will hope. (Matt. 12.18–21)

And,

At that time Jesus declared, "I thank you, Father, Lord of heaven and earth, that you have hidden these things from the wise and understanding and revealed them to little children; yes, Father, for such was your gracious will. All things have been handed over to me by my Father, and no one knows the Son except the Father, and no one knows the Father except the Son and anyone to whom the Son chooses to reveal him. Come to me, all who labor and are heavy laden, and I will give you rest. Take my yoke upon you, and learn from me, for I am gentle and lowly in heart, and you will find rest for your souls. For my yoke is easy, and my burden is light" (Matt. 11.25–30).

This was Christ our King's "leadership style": loving, serving, caring, ministering; never forcing compliance, only seeking to persuade others to love him as he loved them.

When Jesus returns, of course, the time for gentle persuasion will be over. All the important life decisions will have already been made. God's judgment will come swiftly at that point, and it will be final. We will reap the outcome of our decisions—especially our decisions regarding what we have done with Jesus Christ.

SIX

Jesus' World-Changing Mission

It is the baldest commonplace to say the work Jesus proposed to accomplish transcends all the dreams of the boldest imagination.
—Atticus G. Haygood [1]

Jesus founded a worldwide movement, built on his teachings but especially on his own person. That movement is still growing 2,000 years later. Everyone recognizes how unique that is; fewer notice the surprising fact that goes along with it: that he even tried. Who sets out to launch a movement that will reach "to the uttermost parts of the earth"? And who promises he'll be with that movement to the ends of the earth, or to the end of time? (Either of those could be valid translations of his promise in Matthew 28.20.) We're so used to Jesus, we can easily miss seeing what an outrageously massive mission he came to accomplish.

How Did He Know?

For it was undeniably a worldwide movement he came to found. He makes that clear from the start, at his first announcement of the Kingdom of God in Mark 1.14–15. Once he'd accomplished two preparatory steps—his baptism, and his time of prayer and fasting in the wilderness—his first words were, "Repent, for the kingdom

---

[1] Haygood, Atticus G., *The Man of Galilee, 1889* (Chillicothe, OH: DeWard Publishing, 2012), 48.

of heaven is at hand" (see also Matthew 4.17). At the other end of his ministry (Matt. 28.18–20; Acts 1.8), he told his followers to make disciples of all nations, to baptize them, and to teach those disciples to follow his commands. These were *commands*; not just nice, hopeful ideas, but specifically his instructions. This movement was to be his from beginning to end, and it was to be global.

Horace Bushnell says,[2]

> But it is not human, we may safely affirm, to lay out projects transcending all human ability, like this of Jesus, and which cannot be completed in many thousands of years, doing it in all the airs of sobriety, entering on the performance without parade, and yielding life to it firmly as the inaugural of its triumph. No human creature sits quietly down to a perpetual project, one that proposes to be executed only at the end, or final harvest of the world. That is not human, but divine.

Yet Jesus never doubted it would succeed. In Matthew 24.14 he assured his followers, "This gospel of the kingdom will be proclaimed throughout the whole world as a testimony to all nations, and then the end will come." He knew what he'd come to do, and he knew it would be accomplished.

Not an Obvious Undertaking

The long-term success of Jesus' mission could never have been obvious on mere human terms. We've already seen how unlikely his leadership style was: he should hardly even have gained his first followers, humanly speaking, much less the billions who have named his name since then. His style was all wrong—again, looking at it in human terms.

But his strategies were unexpected, too. He ignored politics. He annoyed other leaders much more than he gained any as friends.

---

[2] Bushnell, Horace. *Character of Jesus forbidding his Possible Classification with Men & Christian Nurture*. Kindle Edition. Loc. 378.

He made strange choices for his disciples. Still he went at it with all the calm assurance and authority of a man who knows exactly what he's doing and where it's going to lead, over the course of centuries and all around the globe.

No religious leader ever had such a vision; not until Jesus set the pace. And what a pace he set! His focus was absolute. He had no purpose on earth but to preach and demonstrate the Kingdom, and to provide us the means to enter it, through his death and resurrection. He never swerved to right or left. He stayed with it to the end. His singleness of purpose, in pursuing such a far-reaching vision, is surely unique in the history of human leadership.

How He Could Have Gone Off Course

Consider all the ways he could have let himself be thrown off course, yet never did.

Family. He could have been swayed by his family. He enjoyed time with them, naturally, as well he should have (see John 2.12), perhaps especially since the angel had declared his mother most blessed among women. As eldest son, he would have had definite family responsibilities, too. But he knew whose Son he really was, just as he asked Joseph and Mary in Luke 2.49: "Did you not know that I must be in my Father's house?"

So he pursued his Father's mission, even to the point of letting his earthly family think he'd gone crazy: They "went out to seize him, for they were saying, 'he is out of his mind'" (Mark 3.21). Most of us in that situation would pause and have a talk with our family: "Look, I care for you all, and I care for the family name, which I carry as firstborn. I sure don't mean to embarrass you here. So, tell you what: I'll cool it for a while." But Jesus didn't come to earth for the sake of Mary's or Joseph's name. He came for his heavenly Father's glory, and for those who would follow his Father, just as he explained when he was speaking outside the temple and his mother and brothers came asking to speak with him:

> But he replied to the man who told him, "Who is my mother, and who are my brothers?" And stretching out his hand toward his disciples, he said, "Here are my mother and my brothers! For whoever does the will of my Father in heaven is my brother and sister and mother." (Matt. 12.46–50)

Countrymen. He could have been swayed by his countrymen. They were looking for a political messiah; he refused to have anything to do with that. Even though he came from Israel, ministered in Israel, and gave priority to the Jews, he was just as quick to point out his mission was larger than Israel. In Chapter Four, we looked at Jesus' use of authority among the neighbors he'd grown up with in Nazareth, in Luke 4.16–30. Now let's view the same event from another point of view. He'd just read from the prophet Isaiah, then sat down to teach: "Today this Scripture has been fulfilled in your hearing."

They loved it. "And all spoke well of him and marveled at the gracious words that were coming from his mouth. And they said, "Is not this Joseph's son?" (Luke 4.22).

Their reaction surprises me in view of the Messianic nature of the prophecy he'd read, originally found in Isaiah 61.1–2. He pronounced it fulfilled, and they were willing to believe it. The great promise was fulfilled, right there in their own hearing! But then, they'd known Jesus since his growing-up years. They knew he was different. They'd seen his greatness. Very likely they thought he was making ready to announce his campaign to set Israel free from Rome. So they too, like his family, wanted to claim them for his own. Jesus' mission was larger than that, however: "He said to them, 'Doubtless you will quote to me this proverb, "Physician, heal yourself." What we have heard you did at Capernaum, do here in your hometown as well.'"

They wanted him playing hometown boy, but Jesus let them know it wasn't going to work that way; he wasn't theirs, and they couldn't act like they owned him. So he drew a boundary: "Truly, I say to you, no prophet is acceptable in his hometown."

He could have stopped right there, and the saying might have confused them, but they'd have puzzled it out peacefully enough. Instead he went on:

> But in truth, I tell you, there were many widows in Israel in the days of Elijah, when the heavens were shut up three years and six months, and a great famine came over all the land, and Elijah was sent to none of them but only to Zarephath, in the land of Sidon, to a woman who was a widow. And there were many lepers in Israel in the time of the prophet Elisha, and none of them was cleansed, but only Naaman the Syrian" (Luke 4.23–27).

His point: God cares for others, not just the Jews. Their response to him when he said that? They'd been basking in the light of his hometown greatness, but here their "basking" hit a wall, or you could say it fell off a cliff. Indeed, they actually tried to dump Jesus over a cliff—literally:

> When they heard these things, all in the synagogue were filled with wrath. And they rose up and drove him out of the town and brought him to the brow of the hill on which their town was built, so that they could throw him down the cliff. But passing through their midst, he went away (Luke 4.28–30).

Thus we see that when Jesus had the chance to let hometown loyalties turn him off his path, he widened the path he preached, letting his neighbors know he had come for the whole world.

Propriety. Jesus could have let propriety sway him. He sought righteousness instead. He did what was right, not what others told him was right.

The world has never seen that to the same total degree in any other individual. As we saw in Chapter Four, he set his own moral course, and he expected the rest of us to follow. And yes, he was perfectly willing to offend the keepers of the customs (Luke 7.36–50). Take the Sabbath, for another example. The Jews had it all wrong, he said. The Sabbath was made for man, not man for the Sabbath; and besides, he was Lord of the Sabbath (Mark 2.27–28). In those few simple words—plus repeated demonstrations of his healing grace on Sabbath days—he upended centuries of tradition. He walked his own path. It didn't bother him that others thought he was wrong, except for his being angered and grieved at their hardness of heart, as we saw earlier while looking at Mark 3.5. It was the same hardness that would eventually lead his opponents to nail him to the cross.

Jesus broke with propriety, too, by associating with women, including his close friends Mary and Martha. He broke it triply by conversing with the woman at the well in John 4: She was a woman, a Samaritan, and a sinner. She wasn't the only sinner he spent time with, either. And as always, he did it out of mission-driven love.

Popularity. He could have let *popularity* sway him. It would have been so easy. Jesus came to set up a Kingdom, and Satan tried giving him a shortcut, offering him all the kingdoms of this world (Luke 4.5–8). He refused, knowing it could never be the Kingdom of God on those terms.

But he also passed up opportunities that weren't so obviously wrong—like the time he practically chased some of his followers away.

It happened after he'd fed the 5,000, as recorded in John's account. The crowds loved him for it. The clichéd phrase, "He had them eating out of his hand," was fairly literally true at that point.

Now, how would you or I capitalize on an opportunity like that? Not the way he did. He told them first that they were looking for the wrong thing:

> "Truly, truly, I say to you, you are seeking me, not because you saw signs, but because you ate your fill of the loaves. Do not work for the food that perishes, but for the food that endures to eternal life, which the Son of Man will give to you. For on him God the Father has set his seal" (John 26–27).

Naturally they asked how they could get that bread. He told them they must believe in him. They came back with a question that I'll admit makes no sense to me at all: "So they said to him, "Then what sign do you do, that we may see and believe you? What work do you perform? Our fathers ate the manna in the wilderness; as it is written, 'He gave them bread from heaven to eat'" (John 6.30–31). You'd think they hadn't just seen him provide food from heaven!

But then their questions turned to grumbling, especially among the leaders. He was speaking to them all, though, when he said (John 6.53–54), "Truly, truly, I say to you, unless you eat the flesh of the Son of Man and drink his blood, you have no life in you. Whoever feeds on my flesh and drinks my blood has eternal life, and I will raise him up on the last day." It was exactly the wrong thing to say, if what he'd wanted to do was to build momentum. For after those words, many "turned back and no longer walked with him" (John 6.66). There went a whole crowd of followers! What a lost opportunity!

Jesus knew his mission required truly committed and trained followers, not casual bread-seekers. So he turned and asked his disciples: would they leave, too? Peter spoke for them—and note carefully here what he didn't say. He didn't say he understood Jesus. Rather, he showed he was willing to stay in school with his

Lord: "Lord, to whom shall we go? You have the words of eternal life, and we have believed, and have come to know, that you are the Holy One of God" (John 6.68–69).

Jesus made it challenging, not easy, to follow him. He told a rich young man to sell all his goods if he wanted to follow him (Matt. 19.16–23). In three quick vignettes (Luke 9.57–62) he showed he wouldn't accept followers except on the most serious terms, for as he told one would-be seeker, "No one who puts his hand to the plow and looks back is fit for the kingdom of God."

"Enter by the narrow gate," he told the crowds on the mountainside, "for the gate is wide and the way is easy that leads to destruction, and those who enter by it are many. For the gate is narrow and the way is hard that leads to life, and those who find it are few" (Matt. 7.13–14). Christianity is hard. In fact, following Jesus is only possible because he died for us and lives in us. He carries the load, provided we trust him with it (Matt. 11.25–29).

Is this any way to start a global movement, though—chasing followers away? Who would have dreamed of it? But it wasn't just a matter of leadership strategy. It was about his moral courage, which wouldn't allow him to let go of his integrity one inch to shorten the path toward the Kingdom he'd come to bring.

With all these people leaving him, an ordinary leader would have said, "Oh, nuts!"—however you'd say that in Aramaic—"This isn't working! I'll back off these grandiose dreams and try to do some actual good where I can." Who would have blamed him? It's not as if he saw great results during his time on earth. He planted a tiny seed. It grew, invisibly at first, then just barely perceptibly, until—just as he knew it would (Matt. 13.32), it grew "larger than all the garden plants and [became] a tree, so that the birds of the air come and make nests in its branches." Whatever one's theology of the Kingdom of God, this parable is certainly a great prediction of its manifestation through the worldwide church today.

Never Swayed from His Mission

Family, countrymen, propriety, popularity—any of these could have turned Jesus off course, but none of it did. He would not be distracted, not moved, not even slightly disturbed from his mission. When it came time to "set his face to go to Jerusalem" (Luke 9.51) for his trial and crucifixion, he would not be dissuaded. Not even by his disciples, including Peter, who told him (I paraphrase), "No! Never!" (Matt. 16.21–23). He refused to be turned aside by the villagers in Samaria who rejected him on his way there (Luke 9.52–53). He didn't shrink from the devastating betrayal, massive pain, and brutal execution he knew he soon must suffer.

I could speak at length of Jesus' courage and grace during his trial, where he could easily have called for legions of angels to rescue him, but continued instead in the integrity of his purpose. I could share his words of forgiveness from the cross. These are familiar passages to most Christians. How often, though, do we pause to wonder at the supernatural *consistency* of his character?

In all antiquity there is no courage like his in the face of death. The closest is Socrates, who calmly accepted the decision of the court, and drank the deadly hemlock without a moment's hesitation. He even spoke a word of appreciation for the man who had brought him his poison, and who could not bear to remain and see him drink. "What a charming person!" said Socrates. "All the time I have been here he has visited me, and sometimes had discussions with me, and shown me the greatest kindness—and how generous of him now to shed tears for me at parting!"

It was a great moment of genuine virtue, and I have no desire to take anything from it. But in no way does it compare to Jesus. Socrates suffered no torture before his death and no physical pain after swallowing the poison. He accepted the fate handed him, but other than standing in his integrity he had no choice about it. Jesus, in contrast, designed and crafted his own path to the cross—a path he had started on even before he was born.

He was on a mission to change the world, completely and forever. He did it for joy (Heb. 12.1,2) and to reconcile us to God. He never wavered even a moment on the path. He never doubted it would happen according to plan.

It Worked

And it worked. He set out to found a global movement, and two thousand years later it's going strong. Many people—*too many*—remain unreached with the good news of Christ. But there's no doubt his mission will be accomplished.

So again, my question is, how did Jesus know this unprecedented strategy of his would pay off so well and last so long? We don't often ask this. Looking backward from where we are, we know the answer: He knew because he was God in the flesh, fulfilling a plan that had been put in place before the foundations of the world. That's a perfectly satisfactory explanation, in my book.

Skeptics have a mystery on their hands. They can't deny the effectiveness of Jesus' strategy, but they have no brilliant leader to attribute it to. They have an effect—the worldwide movement of Jesus-followers—without much of a Jesus, not much of a cause, to attribute it to. It seems to me that should bother them more than it does.

Christians know better. We know he came with wisdom, love, brilliance, and yes, effective, world-changing strategy. We know he stuck with it even when there was no human way to see it succeeding. We see his integrity in that, his moral courage.

He knew what he'd come to do. He did it. We're still reaping the benefits all these centuries later.

SEVEN

Jesus, the Man Who Was God

The transcendence of His true humanity, the beauty and completeness of His character, and the holiness and morality of the life He lived; all can only be explained by the testimony of the man Himself: "I and the Father are one" (John 10.30).   —*Philip Schaff*[1]

We were gathered for prayer, our small group in the dormitory at Michigan State. Some Jehovah's Witnesses had been visiting in the dorm, so we were praying about that. Someone asked, "What's the issue with them, anyway?" Our leader answered, "Well, to start with, they don't believe Jesus was God." One of our group members spoke up: "He wasn't." That was the first time he revealed he was a member of The Way International, a small Midwest-centered cult. It was also the first time I as a young Christian learned of the debates over Jesus' deity.

Christian doctrine is clear: Jesus was God in the flesh. We've seen how that reality explains his unique, extraordinary life. No mere human could love as he loved, lead a mission as he led his, or show perfect brilliance as he did. Christianity stands or falls with the doctrine of Jesus' deity. The first defining characteristic

---

[1] Schaff, Philip, *Person of Christ: the Perfection of His Humanity Viewed as a Proof of His Divinity*, Kindle ed. (Hannibal, MO: Granted Ministries Press, 2013), Kindle loc. 130.

of a cult is that it denies Jesus' Godhood, or waters it down so much it retains nothing of the fullness of meaning we find in the Bible.

How do we *know* Jesus was God, though? Years ago I was responsible for training a new Campus Crusade for Christ staff member who had a lot going for him: incredible talent, and more than average Bible background. I've got tremendous respect for him and his ministry today, but at the time, well, he didn't actually have as much going for him as he thought he did. He wasn't terribly sure he needed the training I was taking him through. So I asked him, "Okay, if you're so well prepared already, please answer just one question that's right at the core of Christianity: Where in the Bible do you go to find the truth that Jesus was God?"

He couldn't answer. Jesus' deity one of the most important truths of the Christian faith, but he couldn't tell me why Christians believe it's true. That moment became a turning point in his training, I'm glad to say, because from that point on he knew he still had things to learn. My guess, though, is that if he had trouble answering the question, so would a lot of Christians.

The Bible's clearest statements on it are in the opening verses of the book of John, and in John 8.58, John 10.30, John 14.7–8, Colossians 1.15–20, and the first paragraph of the letter to the Hebrews. It's worth diving into those passages, if only briefly.

The opening verses of John not only tell us it was through "the Word" that the world was created—a clear mark of deity; they actually tell us that "the Word was God." We know from John 1.14–17 that the Word was Jesus himself. Later in John 8.58, Jesus uses for himself the name God gave himself at the burning bush with Moses, and makes a claim to life before his own birth, when he said, "Before Abraham was born, I am." His statement in John 10.30, "I and the Father are one," uses a Greek word that indicates that he and the Father were one in essence, not just (as we might say) "one in spirit." That's why he could tell Phillip in John 14.7–8, "He who has seen me has seen the Father."

We also see Jesus directly involved in creation work, in Colossians 1.15–20, and in Hebrews 1.1–3. These passages also say that Jesus was "the image of the invisible God" (Col. 1.15), the "radiance of the glory of God, the exact imprint of his nature" (Heb. 1.3). No one could be such a close and glorious representation of God but God himself! So there's plenty in the Bible to show that Jesus was more than a man, and nothing less than God in the flesh.

Skeptics have a problem with all this, though. They note that Matthew, Mark, and Luke—called the Synoptic Gospels—are conspicuously missing from this list of clear and obvious statements of Jesus' deity. They claim Jesus' deity was absent in the Synoptics because Christians hadn't quite yet invented that belief, there in the middle to late first century when those books were written. As Bart Ehrman put it in the title of one of his books, it wasn't until years later that "Jesus Became God." Therefore it was only in later-written documents such as John and Hebrews that we see his deity. (Colossians wasn't even written by Paul, they claim, so they find that reference easy to ignore.[2])

The skeptics are wrong, as my friends Rob Bowman and Ed Komoszewski have shown in their very readable *Putting Jesus in His Place: The Case for the Deity of Christ*.[3] The Bible has plenty to say about Jesus as God. Bowman and Komoszewski use a helpful acronym, HANDS, to show that throughout the New Testament,

---

[2] I have focused this book entirely on the Gospels, so I have no need here to enter into any debates over the Epistles, but I find the arguments for Pauline authorship thoroughly convincing. See for example https://crossexamined.org/paul-write-thirteen-letters-attributed/.

[3] Bowman, Robert M. and J Ed Komoszewski. *Putting Jesus in His Place: The Case for the Deity of Christ* (Grand Rapids: Kregel Publications), 2007.

Jesus held the Honors, Attributes, and Names of God; he did the Deeds of God, and he occupies the Seat of God. That is, he is King, just as God is King. So the message of Jesus' deity isn't only found in John, it pervades the entire New Testament.

There's additional evidence of his deity, though, in what Jesus didn't say and didn't do. I was in a series of meetings with a would-be cult leader, of all places, when I discovered one of them: Surprisingly, Jesus never prayed or even spoke the way he told his disciples to pray. A second is even more surprising: The Gospels never say Jesus had the one spiritual character quality he most desired in his disciples. It's missing in his life—or is it? Not if he was God.

Jesus Never Said, "Our Father" (Except When He Told the Disciples to Say It)

His name was John. I met him when he tagged along for a meeting I'd set up to share the gospel with his twenty-something son. I call him a "would-be" cult leader because he had only four or five followers scattered around the U.S.—which made him not much of a leader at all. His beliefs, though, were distorted enough to qualify as a cult.

He and I met five or six times over a period of weeks. The time I spent with him seemed worth it, if it might at least allow me to reach his son with the truth, which he wasn't about to get from his dad. John was convinced that most of the Bible was nothing but "the words of man." Churches were instruments of the devil, he said. He kept repeating, "My Father tells me this," and "My Father has led me to do that." The way he used the phrase, it came across as very intimate with God, very devotional, very positive; yet I had the nagging sense there was something wrong with it. So I did some study—and discovered something I'd never heard preached, and never read in any book or article.[4] Next time I met with him, I brought it to his attention.

"You keep speaking of God as 'My Father,'" I said. "Where would you say that that comes from? Who in the Bible speaks of God that way?"

"Why, the disciples did, of course," he answered confidently.

"I'm sorry, but no," I replied. "I've checked, and they don't. Not even once. Only Jesus spoke of God as '*My* Father.' For everyone else, God was '*Our* Father.'"

John was visibly stunned. I wonder whether some trace of truth might have gotten through to him that day. I'll never know, humanly speaking, because we met only once or twice after that, and I saw no sign of any change in him. He wouldn't allow his son to meet with me again, either.

Meanwhile, though, I was learning more about Jesus and his relationship with the Father. I discovered that not only was Jesus the only one who said, "My Father," he also very carefully avoided saying, "Our Father." Although he instructed the disciples to say it when they prayed (Matt. 6.9–13), he never included himself in that

---

[4]In recent research—finally!—I ran across it in an older source: "Our Lord is frequently depicted in the Gospels as speaking of his Father in relation both to himself and other men. But ... he is never once described as confused in the peculiar relationship in which he stood to God, with that in which men stand to him. The authors of the Gospels have put into his mouth the expressions, 'my Father and your Father,' but never, 'our Father,' as describing a relationship to God common to himself and others. The fourth Gospel sums up this peculiarity on one pregnant sentence, 'My Father and your Father, my God and your God ...'

"Renan tells us that the historic Jesus considered God as standing in the same relation to himself and to every member of the human family. The only difference between Jesus and other men was that he was the first who clearly perceived the reality and nearness of this first relationship. In one word he always viewed God not as "My Father," but as "Our Father."

In Row, Charles Adolphus. *The Jesus of the Evangelists: His Historical Character Vindicated ; or, An Examination of the Internal Evidence for Our Lord's Divine Mission.* (London: Williams & Norgate, 1868), 21–22.

"Our Father" group. Indeed, it's notable how *pointedly* he made the distinction in John 20.17, where he said to Mary, "Do not cling to me, for I have not yet ascended to the Father, but go to my brothers and say to them, 'I am ascending to my Father and your Father, to my God and your God.'" He could so easily have said, "I am ascending to our Father and to our God," but he didn't. Why not?

A simple analogy provides the best explanation. Suppose Father William, a priest in the Episcopal Church, has a son named Will, Jr.; and Will has a good friend in the same church whose name is Jacob. Episcopalians often call their priests "Father," just as Catholics do. So suppose the two boys wanted to know whether it would okay to climb up in the church belfry and take a look around the town from up there.

Do you think Will would say, "Let's go ask our father if it's okay with him?" Not a chance! Will could call him "Father" as his dad, and Jacob could call him "Father" as his priest in the Episcopal tradition, but the word "Father" would mean such different things to the two of them, there'd be no way to rope them together and connect them under the single phrase "our father." Will would certainly say, "Let's go ask *my* father," not, "Let's go ask our father."

The same goes for Jesus. The word "Father" meant something so different to him, it would have been wrong for him to say, "Our Father."

While this isn't proof of his deity, it certainly hints at it pretty strongly. Now, this might not seem like news to many Christians, except for where we see it recorded. Recall that the skeptics claim the Synoptic Gospels lack any reference to Jesus' deity, and that the whole idea was made up years after Jesus walked on earth. Bowman and Komoszewski beat up that theory pretty badly in their book already mentioned above, but here we have even more of a rebuttal, for Jesus' refusal to say "our Father" is characteristic of all four Gospels, not just John. It's especially clear at the end of Luke 2, where Jesus stays behind in Jerusalem while Joseph and Mary travel home to Nazareth. They search for days, and finally find him in the temple. Mary says to him, "Son, why have you treated us so? Behold, your father and I have been searching for you in great distress."

Jesus answers, "Why were you looking for me? Did you not know that I must be in my Father's house?"

Even at age twelve, he wasn't confused. Mary called Joseph his father, but Jesus knew who his Father really was.

Jesus Never Said "Imitate My Faith"

And now we come to one of the most surprising facts about the Gospels. It's been there all along, but I've asked dozens of people, pastors and professors included, and so far I can't identify one who's noticed it. Instead, they ask, "Why have I never seen that before?"

Nowhere in all the Gospels does it ever say that Jesus had faith in God. Use your concordance, your computer, any method you like; you won't find it anywhere in any form whatsoever. Not in the Gospels, and not in the Epistles, either. The book of Hebrews comes closest, in 3.2, where it says Jesus was "faithful to him who appointed him." But that connotes his being consistent and obedient, not his having faith in the Father as we usually think of faith, meaning "belief."

Now, on one level this ought to seem very strange. Jesus urged everyone to have faith in God. He prodded them with it. See Luke 8.25, for example, after he'd calmed the storm on the sea, and asked his disciples, "Where is your faith?" He grieved when he saw faith lacking, as in Matthew 17.17. At home in Nazareth, the people's lack of faith even kept him from performing his usual works of power (Mark 6.5).

So Jesus called us, urgently and constantly, to have faith, yet nowhere does it say he had faith himself. I don't know about you, but I find that striking. What shall we conclude from this? I've been exploring this question with friends, other serious students of the Word, and my most confident conclusion is that it's worth further study. Not everyone agrees on what it means. I'm pretty sure, however, that it means something. What I'm about to suggest here is the best explanation I've uncovered so far.

Why It Has To Mean Something

Let's start by discussing whether it has to mean anything at all. It can be risky, after all, to draw strong conclusions from a description that isn't there. Suppose you were planning to meet a new contact for lunch, and you'd asked him to let you know what he looks like so you can spot him there. "I've got black hair, a full beard, and glasses," he tells you. So you're sitting there at your booth and you see a man with black hear, a full beard, and glasses enter the restaurant, looking around as if to find someone. You wouldn't likely say to yourself, "No, it couldn't be him. This guy's wearing a tie, and he never mentioned that." No, you'd just conclude he didn't think it necessary to say everything about himself.

Suppose on the other hand the man who'd just walked in was six-and-a-half feet tall. Now you might be justified in thinking this was the wrong person: "That couldn't be him; surely he'd have mentioned his height. I'll wait for another dark-haired, bearded man with glasses."

The question comes down to this: Would you have *expected* your contact to have included that trait in his description of himself? Or is it something more incidental, the kind of thing that doesn't need mentioning? Wearing a tie could be considered incidental. But if it turned out the tall man was the one you were there to meet, you'd be very surprised he hadn't mentioned that fact about himself.

Similarly with the Gospels: Would you expect them to mention Jesus' faith? Was his faith more like the man's tie—something

Jesus had, but just didn't merit mentioning? Or was it the sort of thing you really would have expected the Gospels to mention, so that it's really surprising that it isn't there? Does it mean something? I think it does. I think normally we would expect the Gospels to mention Jesus' faith, and that it's surprising that they didn't. I have three reasons for saying so.

First, the New Testament freely and specifically speaks of Jesus' other virtues. We read often of his love, compassion, gentleness, knowledge, wisdom, goodness, forgiveness, humility, joy, prayer, obedience, and patience. It's not just that we *infer* these virtues from the way he lived; the Bible actually *tells us* he had each of them. It's a full list of every human virtue he taught but two. We certainly wouldn't expect him to display repentance; he had absolutely nothing to repent of. That leaves just one major Christian virtue that Jesus is never described as having: faith.

Second, we know that faith was important to Jesus. *Really* important. So important, he mentioned it in his teachings far more often than any other virtue—three times more often than he mentioned love, even.[5]

Third, like Jesus, the Apostle Paul also speaks of his own love, patience, endurance, and other virtues. Unlike Jesus, though, he speaks of his own faith at least a couple dozen times.[6]

Add these three together, and it really seems as though the Gospels ought to have mentioned Jesus' faith. But they didn't. That must mean *something*. But what?

---

[5] Jesus teaches the importance of "faith" in 98 Gospel verses by my count, compared to 32 verses mentioning his teaching of "love." The Gospel of John uses the verb form for "faith," translated "believe" in most English Bibles, but it's the same Greek root word.

[6] Rom. 1.5, 5.1–2, 9.30, 10.6, 12.3, 16.26; 1 Cor. 13.2; 2 Cor. 4.13, 5.7; Gal. 1.23, 2.15–16, 5.5–6; Eph. 2.4–8, 3.12, 4.5, 6.16; Phil. 3.9; 1 Thess. 5.8; 1 Tim. 1.2, 2.7, 4.6, 6.11; 2 Tim. 2.2; Tit. 2.2.

Does It Mean Jesus Didn't Have Faith?

Could it possibly mean that Jesus didn't have faith? How could we say such a thing? He certainly displayed trust in the Father, didn't he? And trust is a very good synonym for faith, in fact better than that, for they both translate the same Greek word. So if Jesus trusted the Father, then he had faith in the Father. The conclusion is unavoidable—except we're still stuck with two striking facts: The Gospels never say he had faith, and this silence on Jesus' faith seems meaningful.

Now, this isn't easy to work through, and I'm well aware that the door remains open for other interpretations. But I can only think of one way to reconcile that with what we know of Jesus' trust in the Father. I think there must have been something different about Jesus' faith or trust in the Father, something so completely different, it places it in a different category than the kind of faith or trust you and I would have.[7] Or in other words, Jesus' faith and trust simply weren't the same thing as ordinary human faith or trust. They were so different that "faith" and "trust" are the wrong words for it.

But it may be that I've started at the wrong end of things. I've told you my conclusion; now I need to explain how I got there. In order to do that, I need to take just a moment to dive deeper into what faith and trust mean for us as believers in God.

The Meaning of "Faith"

Unfortunately too many Christians get the meaning of "faith" wrong. Skeptics and atheists get it even worse: They love calling it a "blind leap" into the unknown, taken for no good reason and

---

[7] I need to re-emphasize that as far as I've been able to discover, the question I'm raising here is relatively new. That means it's wide open to further study which could lead to different conclusions. I welcome that, and I'm open to other possible answers. So far, though, this is the most viable one I've seen that takes all the facts fully into account.

with no evidence backing it up. That's mistaken in all kinds of ways. True faith starts with knowledge, not ignorance.

People come to knowledge of God in different ways. For me it was learning the abundant historical and philosophical evidence we have for the truth of God as revealed in Jesus Christ. For others it's the quality of life they see in other Christians, or the sheer power of God's word, the Bible, speaking to them. All these routes to knowledge work together, and through them believers know God is real.

Still, while faith (properly understood) begins with knowledge, it also includes some element of the unknown, and typically something being put at risk. The day I married my wife, for example, I had faith that she would stay true to me for the rest of our lives. My faith in Sara was based in what I knew of her, which was more than sufficient in my mind, but there was still the possibility I could be wrong. (More than 32 years later that faith is still proving to be well founded, thank God!)

On that day it made sense for me to say I had faith in Sara. On that same day, however, it wouldn't have made sense for me to say, "I have faith that today is August 15, 1987." That was pure knowledge, without any possibility I could be wrong about it.[8]

Faith in God begins with knowledge, but not perfect or pure knowledge. It always involves unknowns, and again, those unknowns typically involve some kind of risk. The classic earthly analogy is boarding an airplane. We know airplanes fly, so we entrust our lives to the equipment and its pilots, despite knowing what could go wrong, flying miles above the ground. Likewise with God, we have more than enough reason to know he's real and that he's

---

[8]Technically, there actually was a chance I could have been wrong. I could have been deluded about the calendar, for example. But in that case it was my own faculties that would be considered unknown, and the faith statement that would make the most sense would be, "I trust my faculties," not, "I trust the date."

trustworthy. Nevertheless, following him fully still means putting something of ourselves on the line.

So for example, we pray with all the faith we can muster, but we still don't know how God will answer, only that he will prove himself faithful as always. We give time and money, counting on God to supply our needs, but often with no idea when or how he'll do that. We go places and say things in his name that could get us ridiculed, mocked, fired, injured, even martyred; still we trust in Christ that he will make it worth any loss we might suffer. We believe in God for eternal life, even though we've never seen that future state for ourselves.

Just today I was talking with a friend who was planning to talk with his lesbian boss about their company's one-sided devotion to the LGBT "Pride" agenda. He could be putting his job on the line. He has plenty of wisdom, and I think he's got a great approach in mind to take to her, so as to say what needs saying while minimizing the risk of repercussions. But he's still walking into a future he can't control and can't even know. That's faith in action.

Our faith (or trust) in God begins with knowledge, knowledge that's sufficient, though it's neither absolute nor perfect. We live with unknowns, which is why we call it *faith* (like my faith in my bride on our wedding day), not *knowledge* (like my knowledge of what day it was).

Jesus' Perfect Knowledge

This all leads us back to a crucial question about Jesus and faith: Did he ever walk into the unknown? There are mysteries here, I'll grant. It's impossible for us to grasp everything it meant that he "emptied himself" at the point of his incarnation (Phil. 2.7). Scholars say he gave up the use and exercise of some portion of his divine power, including his omniscience (having all knowledge). Indeed, Luke 2.52 says he "grew in wisdom and stature," which implies that he didn't always know everything.

Nevertheless we can be quite sure Jesus had perfect knowledge of the Father. Indeed, he was so much like the Father, he could tell Philip, "He who has seen me has seen the Father" (John 14.9). He prayed in John 17.25, "O righteous Father, even though the world does not know you, I know you." He told the Jews in John 8.54–55: "But you have not known him. I know him. If I were to say that I do not know him, I would be a liar like you, but I do know him and I keep his word."

This could explain why Jesus had such a trusting connection with the Father, yet it never be called either faith or trust, because for him, there were no unknowns in his relationship with his Father. He had perfect knowledge. He knew the Father like I knew it was August 15 the day I got married, yet even more surely than that. With such perfect, intimate knowledge, words like "faith" and "trust" simply wouldn't apply. They're the wrong words for it.

If I'm right about this, then it leads to one more way in which Jesus is truly exceptional. Consider Hebrews 1.6, which says "without faith it's impossible to please God." Jesus said he always does what pleases the Father. That could only lead to the conclusion that Jesus had faith—unless he was an exception to the rule stated in Hebrews 1.6. This shouldn't be that hard to accept, if we understand Jesus as the Second Person of the Trinity. Surely he was pleasing to the First Person, the Father, from eternity past. Who would say, though, that he had faith in the Father from eternity past—as if there were even a hint of the unknown in their heavenly relationship?

But Wait!

So am I saying Jesus didn't trust the Father while on earth? Let's be cautious about that, please. Usually if we say someone "doesn't trust someone" it means they *distrust* them, and that's certainly not the case with Jesus and the Father! What I'm saying instead is that we're dealing with limits of language here. We simply do not have a word that accurately describes the unique relationship Jesus had with his Father.[9]

You may want to say, for example, that Jesus displayed trust in the Father when he prayed at Gethsemane. I would suggest that that may be the best word we have for it, but it's still not the *right* word.[10] There *is* no truly right word for it, not in human experience, and therefore not in human language, either. Whatever Jesus was thinking or experiencing as he prayed about his upcoming passion, it was completely different than what we would think or experience in a similar situation. It had to be, considering how different his relationship with the Father was than ours.

Again, am I saying Jesus wasn't faithful? Certainly not! Recall Hebrews 3.2, which says he was "faithful to him who appointed

---

[9] I would argue that this means we don't have a word that fits even analogically (for those who would raise that rather technical issue).

[10] Gethsemane may need further comment here, for arguably there are two different potential readings of Jesus' prayer there. The first reading would take it that Jesus went to the garden with a question he was really hoping could have a different answer: "Can this cup pass from me? Is there no way it might be possible?" He wrestled in prayer until he was assured the answer was still that the Father's answer was still the same, and then he responded in obedience to that confirmed answer. In that case he actually did exercise faith in the Father, in the face of something very significantly unknown to him at the time

The other reading would be that Jesus' prayer throughout the entire hour stood in dynamic tension between what he was feeling and the path he had always known (and still knew) he must take. On this reading, there is no real question, "Can this cup pass from me? Could there be another way?" Instead what we hear there is a cry from Jesus' human nature, crying out his utter aversion toward what he was about to experience, while still saying at every moment, "Not my will, but yours." On this reading, Jesus is not in a state of unknowing. He's only expressing his aversion in a most human manner, along with his continual expression of obedience.

I think the second reading is better reading for two reasons. First, he himself had told the disciples repeatedly that his Passion was coming, and that it was inevitable. Second, I am indeed quite convinced we need an explanation for the striking lack of any mention of Jesus' faith in the New Testament, and this reading explains it far better than the other.

him." I take that to mean that Jesus was perfectly consistent, reliable, and obedient. That's not in question here one bit.

Or am I saying Jesus lacked any other virtue we associate with faith, such as constancy, expectation, wisdom, or love? Again, no. These virtues are just as consistent—much more so, actually—with his perfect knowledge of the Father as they are with faith the way we usually understand "faith."

Or to sum up all such questions, nothing I'm saying here means Jesus lacked anything. I'm only suggesting that "faith," which in human experience always involves unknowns, may be missing from the Gospels' description of Jesus because it's the wrong word to apply to him in his perfectly-knowing relationship with the Father.

God Doesn't Put Faith in God

That's one part of my best explanation for why Jesus is never described as having "faith." The second part is much quicker and easier. I've been leading up to it anyway, as I've been talking about Jesus' perfect knowledge of the Father, for it requires that Jesus himself be God. And does it really make sense for God to have faith in God?

Sure, you and I may say of ourselves, "I have faith in myself that I can do this." We would never say that, though, unless there were something lurking there whispering that we might not be up to it. I don't know many people who would say, "I have faith in myself that I can put my socks on in the morning." The only ones who *would* say it are dealing with some kind of injury or health problem that could put it in doubt. Is anything in doubt with God, though? Is there anything that could possibly lurk in God's background, making him uncertain that he could do what he wills to do? Obviously not! So it just wouldn't make sense for God to say he has faith in God.

The sum of it all, I believe, is that there's just one best way it makes sense for the Bible never to describe Jesus as having faith in the Father. It makes sense if Jesus himself was God.

Making a Case

This isn't absolute proof of Jesus' deity. Proofs like that are hard to come by. As with the "My Father/Our Father" distinction, though, it does contribute to a cumulative case for Jesus as God. Add it in with other indicators, and it makes the whole argument even stronger. There's just no doubt that he was God in human flesh.

EIGHT

Jesus, Friend

The interaction of Christ with his disciples was frank and familiar, yet inspiring reverence and awe. They both loved and adored him as their Friend and Lord, and put their whole trust in him as their Saviour. He called them "friends." —Philip Schaff[1]

Jesus, Friend

You'd think there could be nothing left to astonish us in Jesus after all this, but there is. Think of a great leader you admire from afar, or a celebrity you'd most love to spend time with. Imagine being on a first-name basis with them. I've had the honor and privilege of knowing a couple of prominent leaders that well. And I've discovered there remains some distance from "first-name basis" to "true friends." That's a smaller, more privileged circle yet. But Jesus, the leader of all leaders, the Man who was literally perfect, master of humanity and of all the universe, includes us in that circle. He calls us his brothers and friends. What could a man of his greatness want to do with such small, flawed people as us?

If that seems like an easy question, on one level it is: he is God, and God is love. He created us for fellowship with him. That's

---

[1] Schaff, Philip, *Person of Christ: the Perfection of His Humanity Viewed as a Proof of His Divinity*, Kindle ed. (Hannibal, MO: Granted Ministries Press, 2013), Kindle loc. 879.

straight Christian doctrine, one of the very first things Christian parents teach their kids, impossible to miss in even the simplest, briefest study of God. So it's easy for us to get used to it.

Imagine not being used to it, though. Picture James or Jude, Jesus' younger half-brothers, growing up with a perfect big brother—morally and spiritually perfect, that is. Jesus might have made some kinds of mistakes—cutting or fastening a board wrong, maybe—but he never lied, never acted selfishly, never dishonored his heavenly Father in any way.

Come to think of it, imagine what it was like for Mary or Joseph: "Honey, I thought parents were supposed to teach their kids how to love one another. Why do I get the sense this one is teaching us?" They knew the answer, and yet I still can't help but think how unsettling—disturbing, even—that must have been. Who wants to raise a child like that? The angel had called Mary "Blessed among women." Surely at times she must have thought, "Yes, this is a blessing, raising Jesus, but I'll never get used to it."

Back to James and Jude. Don't you think there must have been times when they said to Jesus, "You think you're so perfect!" Someday in heaven I want to ask them how Jesus answered. (It's another scene I can't quite picture.) They must have felt envious, even intimidated. Surely they must have baited him, trying to get him to slip up. Just as surely, though, Jesus kept loving them persistently. Even his great love didn't fully get through to them until much later, though, because we know his family members didn't accept him as Savior until after his resurrection (John 7.5). Could it be they were put off by his perfection? Intimidated, maybe? Who wouldn't be?

And yet many followed Jesus gladly during his earthly ministry, and after he rose from the grave, James and Jude put all that aside and followed him, too. And so it was that near the end of his earthly life, Jesus spoke one of the most astonishing words in the whole Bible:

> "This is my commandment, that you love one another as I have loved you. Greater love has no one than this, that someone lay down his life for his friends. You are my friends if you do what I command you. No longer do I call you servants, for the servant does not know what his master is doing; but I have called you friends, for all that I have heard from my Father I have made known to you. (John 15.12–15)

He called them friends. He calls *us* friends. Jesus is great beyond imagining, yet he lets himself be approachable. He comes to us with the greatest of love, the love that lays down its life for friends! God, who is so far beyond our upstretched arms' reach, came down to *us*, far enough down to wash his friends' feet.

Not everyone loved him in return, obviously. I wonder whether they might have wanted a less perfect friend, one who would make them feel good for who they were in themselves. Jesus would have nothing of that. He wanted us instead to feel good for who we are in relation to God.

The Humility of Accepting His Love

For we dare not forget that it is Jesus' greatness, not ours, that draws him to us and us to him. We want to be good enough for God. We want God to be *proud* of how good we are. It's such a strong impulse, it's been Christianity's favorite heresy from the very beginning. We call it *legalism*, and it's at the center of all the cults, along with their denials of Jesus' deity. It's because of Jesus' great love, not ours, that he declares us friends. "We love," says 1 John 4.19, "because he first loved us." Everything good in us, including any love we have to give, has its source in God through Jesus Christ. Non-believers share in God's goodness through common grace, the goodness of God expressed in all creation. Believers receive so much more, though, through God's special grace in Christ Jesus: friendship, life, and adoption into his family.

We may want Jesus to love us because we're lovable, but he won't do that. He loves us instead because he is perfect love. This is great news to the humble, but it's bound to bother everyone who wants to think they're loved on account of their own goodness. That's why I wonder whether Jesus' opponents really might have wanted a less perfect friend, someone who might even look up to them a little bit, who'd throw in a bit of admiration along with his love. If so, it would be the same story that's playing out in the lives of many who reject him today.

He Calls Us Friends

But we know that not everyone was put off by his perfections, and that's a wonder, too. Usually we shun "perfect" people as insufferable—those who act like they know everything that matters, who are to rebuke anyone who disagrees with them. That's not the kind of person people normally want to follow, and certainly not one whom others would willingly die for—especially not years after he himself had died! Jesus' perfection couldn't have been a put-on. It had to have been real. It had to have been capped with total love, for only that could have explained so many following him so gladly.

And yes, he welcomed his followers as friends. That includes rogue characters like Peter, who denied him; and James and John, who thought they should be the greatest, and even got their mom to carry the message for them. It included friends like Saul of Tarsus, who had devoted his life to trying to kill Jesus' other friends.

Friends—Not Buddies

We must not be mistaken, though. "Friends" doesn't equal "buddies." For he also said, "You are my friends if you do what I command you." It's another unexpected saying, leaving us in the same strange territory we've been walking throughout this whole book. He invites us to be his friends, but only on his terms, and exactly on his terms. In any other relationship, that kind of expectation would be absolutely wrong. It would be abusive, dysfunctional to the extreme. But not with Jesus, the only one ever who could express perfect power and perfect love at the same time.

I suspect C. S. Lewis knew something of this strange, overpowering, even overbearing aspect of Jesus' love, and wrote of it in a letter to a former pupil, on March 26, 1940:[2]

> Now the truth is, I think, that the sweetly-attractive-human-Jesus is a product of 19th century scepticism, produced by people who were ceasing to believe in His divinity but wanted to keep as much Christianity as they could. It is not what an unbeliever coming to the records with an open mind will (at first) find there. The first thing you find is that we are simply not invited to speak, to pass any moral judgement on Him, however favourable: it is only too clear He is going to do whatever judging there is: it is we who are being judged, *sometimes* tenderly, sometimes with stunning severity, but always *de haut en bas*.[3] (Have you ever noticed that your imagination can hardly be forced to picture Him as shorter than yourself?)
>
> The first real work of the Gospels on a fresh reader is, and ought to be, to raise very acutely the question, "Who or What is this?" For there is a good deal in the character which, unless He really is what He says He is, is not lovable or even tolerable. If He is, then of course it is another matter: nor will it then be surprising if much remains puzzling to the end. For if there is anything in Christianity, we are now approaching something which will never be fully comprehensible.

---

[2] Lewis, *C. S. Letters of C.S. Lewis*, ed. W.H. Lewis. Revised and enlarged edition (San Diego: Harcourt Brace, 1993), 344–345

[3] Literally, from top to bottom; meaning that one thinks one is superior to the other.

A Love Like No Other

We sing at churches of Jesus' matchless love, and rightly so, but do we understand how differently he loves? For example: does he ever show any sign that he wants to be *liked*? I raise that question advisedly, for there's a difference between loving a person and liking him. Liking is more a matter for peers. Psychologists who study likability know that one of the quickest routes there is by asking someone to help you with some project, some need; even to pick up a piece of paper you've dropped. It sets the person at ease, marking you very quickly as equal and human in some sense. No one likes the person who is always better than everyone else.

So "liking" Jesus is very likely the wrong word for it. And what about being comfortable with him? It could never be on account of our sharing any equality with him; it could only be the comfort of knowing he loves and cares for us as only God can do. "Look at the lilies of the field," he says, and he tells us the Father will watch over us. "Come to me, all who labor and are heavy laden," he also says. He who will "give you rest," also says, "Take my yoke upon you, and learn from me, for I am gentle and lowly in heart, and you will find rest for your souls. For my yoke is easy, and my burden is light" (Matt. 11.28–30). This is love unlike any we experience anywhere else. The closest parallel is that of parent for child, but it's only a parallel; no parent, not even the best, really stands in the place of God.

Jesus calls us to love him as the one who's absolutely in charge. Look through the rest of the New Testament and you'll find that even though Jesus called his followers "friends," they still called themselves "bondservants," showing how clearly they recognized his kingship. Paul describes himself that way at the start of many of his letters. So does James, Jesus' half-brother. And they considered it total privilege to carry that title. Paul spoke it brilliantly:

Indeed, I count everything as loss because of the surpassing worth of knowing Christ Jesus my Lord. For his sake I have suffered the loss of all things and count them as rubbish, in order that I may gain Christ and be found in him, not having a righteousness of my own that comes from the law, but that which comes through faith in Christ, the righteousness from God that depends on faith—that I may know him and the power of his resurrection, and may share his sufferings, becoming like him in his death, that by any means possible I may attain the resurrection from the dead (Phil.3.8–11).

Of all the great mysteries of Jesus' excellence, sometimes I think his love must be the greatest. It has its frankly intimidating side to it, I'll admit. Like Peter in John 6.68–69, though, I will follow him, for he alone has the answer. He alone is God, and the fullest revelation of God. He alone has the words of eternal life. I can't grasp his love completely, but I can still accept it gladly and give him thanks. His love is for you and me, after all. God loved us enough, says that familiar verse John 3.16, to send his only begotten Son, that whoever believes in him would never perish but have eternal life. That life begins when we believe, and our experience of his love starts then, too. Sure, it's not like any human love; not when it comes from the Ruler of the universe. It's far better, more giving, more secure, and more faithful, just as God himself is greater than any human.

The Total Supremacy of Jesus

And now we approach the end of Part One, our fresh look at Jesus' astonishing uniqueness. I haven't even mentioned the best of it yet: his sacrificial death and magnificent resurrection. I've saved that for Part Three, where it fits better, as you'll see when you get there. But we've already covered enough to see that Jesus is one of a kind, an individual who astonishes at every turn.

His love is unmatched in all history and all literature. His ethical goodness is unparalleled in all history, and even in the greatest authors' imaginations. His teaching methods may look simple, but you can't call a teacher "simple" who gives each person *exactly* what he needs; who never gets the least bit flustered, much less stumped, when the best scholars of the day also happen to be his chief adversaries, constantly trying to trip him up.

He remained absolutely rock solid on mission, when so many people and cultural forces were trying to knock him off course. That's integrity, and it also shows a supernatural awareness of a purpose that would grow and flow down centuries. He assumed authority like no one else has, before or since, and proved his qualifications for it. He founded the world's most successful millennia-long movement, and did it while breaking multiple leadership "rules," only to make up for it with his unmatched wisdom, trustworthiness, and love. He lived as God in the world, and his followers never thought to challenge whether he was fit to do so.

In short, he lived the one completely perfect human life.

Skeptics talk about religion being something people turn to for comfort. That's true enough at times. Often, though, it's anything but that. Remember: Jesus lived a completely perfect human life. There's something truly awesome there; *awesome* in the original sense of *invoking fear—fear coupled with reverence, that is.* It would be so easy, if Jesus had never lived, to give ourselves a pass for our imperfections, saying, "No one could possibly be perfect, anyway." Jesus took that away from us. There's no excuse left. There's no comfort there. We have to find it in his grace instead.

I said earlier I can hardly stand the thought of what it would mean to be as giving, as loving, as other-oriented as our Savior. It's too out of reach, too far beyond me. I can't even conceive of what it would be like spending time with such a person. No one alive comes within miles of that standard. Jesus lived a life beyond our reach. We can only approach him on our knees. Thank God we can at least come to him that way! And yet he calls his followers his friends. There are times when that strikes me as the most surprising thing of all, in this great, beautiful, majestic story of our Lord Jesus Christ.

But What If It Isn't True?

But what if it's just a story? What if that's all it is? There are lots of stories; *what if this one isn't true?*

It's time now to transition to Part Two, which will focus on answering that one great question, the one that's been lurking behind everything I've said so far: What if it isn't real? What if it's all just a legend?

Now, maybe you're not asking that. Maybe you don't have the slightest doubt of it. It could even be that no one you care about does, either. In that case, you could skip ahead to Part Three. I don't recommend it, though. For one thing, Part Two builds on the unique message of Part One, carrying it forward to form a whole new way of looking both at Jesus Christ and at reasons for confidence in Christ.

There are plenty of books and hordes of websites explaining how we can be confident in Christianity. I'm all for that. May they increase more and more! I list several in the Resource Guide at the end of this book, and I hope you'll study them all. You'll find that the approach I take here is different than most, though, and I think refreshingly so, as it's based almost entirely on the character of Christ as we read it in the Gospels. How does his character demonstrate his reality, you wonder? Read on!

Second, if you think no one in your life has any doubts about Jesus, you're almost certainly wrong. The odds are against it. Children are the prime example (though the same applies to classmates, co-workers and friends, just in different ways). They grow up believing what their parents say, but only for a few years, and then they reach an age to ask questions. They encounter other beliefs on social media, in traditional media, and in school. You might try to protect them from that, but they'd still see it on billboards you drive by on the road. Their questions deserve answers. Part Two will equip you to give some of those answers.

Third, I think you'll find Part Two easier, more familiar, less technical, and possibly even *more fun* than any reasons for faith you may have read. All you need to know is what the Bible says, plus some common sense about human nature, plus some really fascinating information I'll tell you about the skeptics' theories of the story of Jesus.

It all begins with the easiest point in the whole world. There is a story of Jesus. It comes in four closely related versions: Matthew,

Mark, Luke, and John. And stories always come from somewhere. *Where did this one come from?*

PART TWO

Too Good To Be False

PART TWO

Too Good To Be False

For centuries now, skeptics have been trying one way after another to portray the gospels as legends. Christian scholars have answered in multiple ways, and successfully, too, as far as I'm concerned. Naturally the skeptics disagree with them, so the dispute continues. I'm hoping my contribution here in Part Two will help persuade some of them, while also building believers' confidence in the Gospels' historic truth.

Christian scholars already have strong responses to skeptics' legend theories; this book just adds more to an existing body of answers.[1] The main issue: The Gospels, along with associated material in the rest of the material in the New Testament, were written too soon after the events. Legends don't just spring up overnight, especially not legends with as much solid substance as we have in Jesus' resurrection accounts. It's even more implausible when (as skeptics suppose) there's no reality behind them to fertilize their growth.

For example, there were Elvis sightings soon after his death became publicly known. But no one who "saw" him said they sat down and had a meal with him. No one came forward with Elvis's

---

[1] At times I'll refer to legend "theories" instead of "theory," since it comes in more than one version, but the variations share enough in common that it's also generally accurate to interchange that with simply "theory."

own explanation for how he happened to show up alive again. And though the mood in America was ripe at the time for "glimpses" and trace "sightings," nothing in our culture could possibly have hinted at an actual *reason* for him to rise from death, or even to fake his death and allow such glimpses. Over time, therefore, all thought of Elvis's being alive has dissolved into nothing.

Jesus' resurrection was completely different. There was a theological basis for it in the Scriptures and in his identity as God's Son. The disciples reported eating with him on several occasions after his resurrection. They had long conversations with the risen Jesus, again adding to the substance of the reports. Many of the disciples died for their belief in his resurrection, a belief they couldn't honestly have been mistaken about, in view of the concrete nature of their belief and the variety and depth of their direct contact with him. (Mass hallucinations just don't happen that way.) If they'd reported it wrongly, and it wasn't an honest mistake, it would have had to have been a lie. And while skeptics just love pointing out that people die for lies all the time, we never find people dying for lies they *made up themselves.* Yet every one of the disciples who faced the choice to die or else recant their belief in Christ, chose death.

And for one further nail in the legend theory's coffin, we return to the fact that legends don't spring up so quickly as this one must have (if that's what it was). The earliest report of Jesus' resurrection isn't in the Gospels, it's in 1 Corinthians 15.3–7. Everyone agrees 1 Corinthians was written before any of the Gospels. Not only that, but there's widespread agreement, even among secular scholars, that the phrase, "I delivered to you what I first received" in 1 Cor. 15.3 refers to a statement Paul likely "received" within three to five years of Jesus' death.[2] If the resurrection was legend,

---

[2] Paul received it either on his first visit to Jerusalem, three years after his conversion, or his second visit fourteen years later. See Galatians 1.18–2.1.

it grew up at unbelievable speed—much too fast for any legend to develop. Which makes that theory very hard to believe.

All these are reasons we can count on the truth of the gospels, and they're solid on their own. They all share one feature in common, though: You won't get anywhere with them without spending serious time studying what scholars know about the New Testament manuscript, plus the lives of the disciples beyond the Gospels and the book of Acts. (Not that this information is hard to find. My favorite source for it is J. Warner Wallace's immensely informative and readable *Cold-Case Christianity.)*

But what if the Gospel accounts had their own proofs within them? Skeptics say you can't use the Bible to prove the Bible. Maybe so. But I say that you can use the Bible *plus a little bit of common sense* to show that the skeptics' legend theories can't be true. And we've already laid the groundwork for it. Part One supplies half of the answer. All we need now is to know something of the skeptics' theories of this supposed legend. The conclusion, I trust you will agree, is firm: *Jesus is too good to be false.*

It all starts with the story of Jesus—the same thing we've been dealing with from the beginning here. Now we'll begin looking at the skeptical challenge. Naturally, the tone will change as we shift toward taking a close look at what skeptics think of Jesus. It's only for the next chapter or two, though, and it's in service of a good cause: showing that the story of Jesus isn't just a great story, but a story we can be confident is true.

NINE

The Skeptical Challenge

We will demand of those who deny or doubt that Jesus really lived to ac-
count to us for the existence of the character.   *—Atticus G. Haygood* [1]

Whatever disputes Christians and skeptics may have, we agree at
least on this much: There is a story of Jesus. Not only that, but the
story came from somewhere.

Doesn't seem like much of a start, does it? But it's at least something—and in a very real sense it's all we need. All it takes from
there is filling in the details. Where did this astonishing, unique
story come from? From the real life of a real person who really
walked the earth? Or from the misty beginnings of a legend that
grew up around who-knows-what?

Let's not rush into it too quickly, though. There is a story of
Jesus. We can treat it simply as that for now, which is fine both
for Christians and non-believers. The old hymn does say, after all,

> Tell me the stories of Jesus
> I love to hear.
> Things I would ask him to tell me
> If he were here.

---

[1] Haygood, Atticus G., *The Man of Galilee, 1889* (Chillicothe, OH: DeWard
Publishing, 2012), 6.

I'm satisfied the story is true, of course. By viewing it simply as story, though, we can give skeptics the greatest benefit of the doubt. For simplicity's sake we can treat it as just a *single* story for starters—one story, that is, presented in four different variations, the four Gospels. Some skeptics may object to that approach, saying there are multiple contradictions among the Gospels. I think they'll see as we proceed, though, that these alleged contradictions make little to no difference to the work at hand. I'll return to that later on, at any rate, to show how we can view them most reasonably in light of the rest of this discussion. Whatever problems skeptics think these contradictions cause, it should become plain by then that they're nothing compared to the problems skeptics themselves must face in a four-fold view of Christ's character.[2]

We can even set aside (for now) the question of whether the story's miracles are true. I suspect by now you've noticed that in my discussion of Jesus' uniqueness in Part One, I barely mentioned his miracles. That's because we're already used to seeing Jesus' greatness in them, and my purpose has been to focus on truths we're not as familiar with. There's a side benefit, too, to keeping miracles on the back burner: We don't have to ask skeptics to believe any of the miracles up front. They're not essential to the case I'm making here, so we can set them aside for the time being. All we need explore is whose explanation of the story makes sense, given what the story says about Jesus' *character*.

We do have to ask the skeptics to return the favor, of course. It would be jumping the gun for them to say the Gospels must be false just because they have miracles in them. If that's their view of it, they've decided the question before they've even considered the evidence, which isn't very intellectually responsible. I trust we can count on better from them.

---

[2] I believe these alleged contradictions can be resolved, but that's not essential to our work here for the time being.

Backstories

So far so good, then. We have the story of Jesus in its basic out-lines, just as I presented it in Chapter One. Now, we also know that every story also has a backstory, a story-behind-the-story, that helps explain both how the story came to be and how believable the story is. For example, I have a story about how I helped the world-famous singer Sting find his lost contact lenses in a ski-re-sort locker room. We were there together, he lost his lens, I helped him find it, he thanked me, we talked for a while, and we went on our ways. That really happened. It's a true story.[3]

But surely that leaves you gasping with questions. *How did you meet Sting in a locker room, Tom?* I'm so glad you asked! He was the lead singer with The Police band at that time. I was traveling with the band on their first North American tour as their chief sound engineer—stadiums, arenas, you name it, we were there. We had a couple days off, so we hopped on our private jet for a quick trip to Vail. We'd been relaxing in the sauna together when he lost his lens, and from there you know the rest of the story.

And of course, you know not a word of that is true. You're even wondering if you should believe the part of it that I promised you *was* true. If the backstory is unbelievable, the main story must be doubtful, too.

So here's the truth. (This time it really is true. I have no need to play tricks on you a second time.) I was at a singles' conference in Keystone, Colorado. I don't remember why I decided to take a shower in the locker room, but I did. While changing clothes I noticed another man there, looking for a lost contact lens. I helped

---

[3] It's true, that is, except for one possible problem: I didn't ask him his name. He did say he was a member of *The Police* band, and from my view of the band's photos, he did look like Sting, but it's possible it could have been Stewart Copeland or Andy Summers instead. All three of them were there at the time, at any rate.

him search for it, along with others who were in there. It wasn't showing up, so after several minutes he told us all, "Let it go. It's okay, you can forget about it." I objected, "No, these things cost money!" (Once I found out who he was, I had to laugh at myself over that. *Boy, did he not care about paying for a contact lens!)*

Anyway, I kept on looking and I found it. He was grateful enough to chat a while. I'd noticed his British accent, so naturally I asked him what he was doing in the States. That's when I found out who I was talking to.

Is that any more believable now? Sure, it's still pretty crazy, I know, but it doesn't sound impossible like the first version I told you. And I'll say it one more time: It really did happen!

When the Flyleaf Doesn't Fit the Story

Backstories have a big impact on how believable stories can be. It works the other way around, too: Stories can affect the believability of a backstory. I'll stay on the musical theme for my next example.

Imagine your brother-in-law is a world-renowned concert pianist. One day you ask him what it's like being a great and famous musician. He pulls a book off his bookshelf, and says, "Here, read this. It's a novel about life as a concert pianist. These authors get it. They know exactly what it's like to be on the road as a classical musician. They know the ups and downs, the crowds, yet also the loneliness that come with being the soloist, the star. They've got an especially good handle on what it's like to be a *classical* soloist, rather than a rock star, say, or even a star athlete. And it's as if they know the feel of the ivory under the hands. They have the gift of telling what it's like—what it actually *feels like*—to have great music flowing out of your soul."

So you open it up, look at the flyleaf, and read that the book was co-authored by a pro hockey player from Calgary and his business manager. You'd drop that book so fast it'd hurt your toes. You might still believe the story was good (the book itself, that is), since you have your brother-in-law vouching for it. But you'd know for sure there was something wrong with the backstory—the note on the flyleaf explaining where the book had come from.

Or imagine yet another version of the flyleaf: that the book had been written by a musical *savant,* a prodigy whose piano skills had impressed the entire world, but whose reading and writing skills had only reached third-grade level. You might still feel confident in the contents of the book, but you'd have good reason to believe someone else wrote it.

The Corrupted Flyleaf Backstory

There's a strong parallel here to our question about the skeptics and the Gospels. We could phrase it this way: If the Gospels had a flyleaf like a modern hardcover book, and if that flyleaf had the authors' pictures and bios on it, what would it show there? What actually *belongs* on the Gospels' flyleaf? Where did the Gospels come from? Different scholars would have different versions, so which should we believe? Should we think of the Gospels' traditional flyleaf as obviously fake, like the hockey guys or the *savant* writing about life as a classical concert pianist? Or would it be more real and believable than that?

The believer's answer is quite simple: This flyleaf would have four pictures on it. Two of them would be of Matthew and John, apostles and direct eyewitnesses of Jesus. A third would be of Mark, who reported mostly what Peter the apostle told him. The final photo would be of Luke, who traveled with Paul and did all kinds of independent investigation into the life of Christ, just as he says in the first several verses of his Gospel and the book of Acts.

Now remember (for the sake of skeptics, at least), we're just looking at the Gospels *as stories;* for now, that is. We can wait a while before pronouncing on whether they're true or not. As long as no one jumps the gun, though, insisting, "No! It can't be true! It's got miracles in it!" then Christians' version of the flyleaf fits the Gospels' contents. That's a definite mark in the Gospels' favor, though not enough on its own to establish them as true, at least not on that basis, not yet. We must keep going.

The skeptics' flyleaf for the Gospels would look completely different. Atheist *extraordinaire* Richard Dawkins tweeted,[4] "Of course the legend of Jesus was invented like those of all gods." So there'd be no author bios to display, no clear photos, nothing but a vague and hazy story of a legend arising somehow somewhere in the centuries following Jesus' life. Again, though, the question applies: "Does this flyleaf—the skeptics' explanation of where the Gospels came from—fit the content of the books?" To answer that, we need to fill in some details. What do skeptics actually say about who wrote these accounts of Jesus and how those persons came to write it? Then once we know that, we can ask, does their flyleaf fit the contents? You'd be surprised how seldom that question gets raised.

The Skeptics' Gospel Flyleaf

What the skeptics typically say, in short, is that the Gospels are a hodgepodge, compiled by unknown authors who never knew Jesus and probably didn't know any of his followers, either. These unknown persons set down "traditions" they'd received—traditions we can't trace in detail. All we know for sure is that the whole thing was overrun with processes guaranteed to utterly distort the truth.

And since you've read this far in the book, you're probably already thinking, "That's nuts. A great story with a great character like Jesus could *never* have come to be by such a mixed-up

---

[4] Richard Dawkins, Twitter, April 10, 2013, https://twitter.com/richarddawkins/status/322050796768333824.

process!" If so, you've got it—that's the point. Jesus is literally too good to be false!

I've only given you the bare bones here, though, so you'd be unwise to draw strong conclusions so quickly. Besides, the skeptics are nowhere near agreeing with you yet, so it would be wise to be patient with them, and also with me, as I proceed to lay out the case for them. It's good to know who's saying these things about the story of Jesus, anyway, and how they're saying it. You may find that skeptics' problems are actually worse than you thought, and certainly worse than *they* thought.

But let's get back to the skeptics' backstory. The way I summarized their account of the Gospels' distortions, it might sound so bad you'd wonder if I was exaggerating. I'm not. In fact, at least one skeptical scholar thinks most people *understate* how much distortion has been introduced into the legend of Jesus.

> When the popular cultural context within which stories about Jesus were first told or retold are taken into account, it becomes apparent that they are likely to be characterized by far more creativity, improvisation, idiosyncrasy, and inconsistency then has hitherto been assumed by most New Testament scholars. ... Most scholars have tended to underestimate or pass over the potential for mythmaking in the initial years of movements that made claims, of one kind or another, about the figure of Jesus.[5]

"Far more creativity," he says, meaning far more invention, sending the story further and further from reality. More "improvisation," too, which I take to mean something like making things up on the spot. "Idiosyncrasy" implies people everywhere devising their own different versions of the story, and "inconsistency" suggests there's nothing much to tie it all together. The result: "mythmaking."

---

[5] J. Meggitt, "Popular Mythology in the Early Empire and the Multiplicity of Jesus Traditions," in *Sources of the Jesus Tradition: Separating History from Myth*, edited by R.J. Hoffman, 55–80 (Amherst, NY: Prometheus Press, 2010), 55.

The Gospels must quite be a mess, based on that! Which is exactly what the skeptics tend to think. They don't agree on everything, mind you. They differ on details. But they do tend to run in sync on the general outline of the backstory. Liberal Episcopalian bishop John Spong, for example, said Jesus' birth accounts were[6]

> perhaps . . . designed to cover some unprotected flag of the Christian story. Maybe there were rumors about Jesus' paternity. . . . The suggestion that a scandal needed to be covered up is apparent in a number of places in the New Testament. . . . At the very least that it is not an original part of the Jesus story. Rather, it is a late–developing, interpretive tradition that obviously incorporates symbols that were never meant to be literalized. Virgin births were a familiar tool in the ancient world to explain the extraordinary qualities of a leader.

Best-selling author Reza Aslan says similarly,[7]

> The Gospels are not, nor were they ever meant to be, historical documentation of Jesus' life. They are not eyewitness accounts of Jesus' words and deeds, recorded by people who knew him. They are testimonies of faith composed by communities of faith and written many years after the events they describe.

Atheist Kris Komarnitsky agrees,[8]

> Christianity started off with a bang. Immediately after Jesus' obscure burial there was a swirl of rationalizations, individual hallucinations, collective enthusiasm, vying for positions of authority, and scriptural interpretation.

---

[6] John Shelby Spong, *Jesus for the Non-Religious* (New York: HarperCollins, 2007), 31.

[7] Reza Aslan, *Zealot: The Life and Times of Jesus of Nazareth.* 1st ed. (Random House, 2013), Kindle loc. 214.

[8] K.D. Komarnitsky, *Doubting Jesus' Resurrection: What Happened in the Black Box?* (Stone Arrow Books, 2009), Kindle loc. 1827.

"Rationalizations" and "hallucinations," he says, adding to Spong's "late-developing, interpretive tradition ... never meant to be literalized" and Aslan's "never meant to be historical." Not everyone goes with the "hallucination" part of the theory, but still, it all fits the general outline: The Gospels are a mass of errors, rationalizations, and distortions.

Bart Ehrman

No skeptic, though, writes and sells more books than Bart Ehrman. A professor of New Testament at the University of North Carolina, Ehrman says he was once a believer in Christ. His faith was rocked, however, when he began discovering "discrepancies" in the Gospels. He's troubled by the problem of evil, too: how a good and powerful God could permit evil and suffering in the world. So he's turned away from Christ and become a crusading (and best-selling) skeptic. His books include *How Jesus Became God: The Exaltation of a Jewish Preacher from Galilee; Jesus, Interrupted: Revealing the Hidden Contradictions in the Bible (And Why We Don't Know About Them); Misquoting Jesus: The Story Behind Who Changed the Bible and Why;* and *Jesus Before the Gospels: How the Earliest Christians Remembered, Changed, and Invented Their Stories of the Savior.* He summarizes our flyleaf question well enough in *How Jesus Became God:*[9]

> Anything you know about Jesus, or think you know, has come to you from a source—either someone has told you, or you have read what someone has written. But where did these people get their information, what makes them authorities, and why should you think they are right? Every story about Jesus (or any other historical figure) either is historically accurate (something he really said or did) or is made up, or is a combination of the two.

---

[9] Bart D. Ehrman, *How Jesus Became God: the Exaltation of a Jewish Preacher from Galilee* (New York, NY: HarperOne, 2015), Kindle loc. 1331.

That's a great statement of the question *"Where did the story come from?"* For Ehrman, the most believable answer is that the Gospels are almost completely unbelievable. The disciples needed a messiah, so they created one, and creeds to go with him. There's a great example in Philippians 2.5–11, says Ehrman—a creed they began framing soon after Jesus died. They'd really thought Jesus was the hoped-for one who would free Israel, but then his death squashed those hopes to nothingness. Still, though, squashed hopes can always rise again in resurrected—albeit corrupted—form. Shortly, we'll see how some scholars think that's what happened in early Christianity. For now, let's see how Ehrman explains the way the Jesus legend grew into a form that the real, original "Jesus" never would have recognized:[10]

> The early Christian "witnesses" to Jesus had to persuade people that Jesus really was the messiah from God, and to do that they had to tell stories about him. So they did. They told stories about what happened at the end of his life—the crucifixion, the empty tomb, his appearances to his followers alive afterward. They also told stories of his life before those final events—what he taught, the miracles he performed, the controversies he had with Jewish leaders, his arrest and trial, and so on.

So far, so good. Ehrman isn't implying (yet) that the stories were false. You might be surprised to hear it, but skeptical scholars tend to agree the disciples had "resurrection experiences" after Jesus' death. They thought they saw Jesus alive, maybe his ghost or his spirit, or who knows what? But it wasn't real, or so say the skeptics.

Anyway, Jesus' followers armed themselves with stories, and oh, what stories they were! Especially when they started getting passed around from city to city. They grew, and they grew, until finally Jesus

---

[10] Ibid, Kindle loc. 1367.

"became God," in Ehrman's words. The tales were spread by word of mouth, naturally, as literacy rates were very low. And everyone knows what happens to word-of-mouth stories: They come out different as time goes on. Ehrman is particularly fond of the Telephone Game—he brings it up in several of his books. It's the game kids play at parties, where they sit in a circle and the first child whispers something in the next child's ear, that child repeats it to the next, and around the circle it goes. When it comes back to the first child again, it's changed so much that everyone gets a great laugh out of it.

So this, says Ehrman, is how the Gospels came to be. But it's actually worse than that:[11]

> Imagine playing telephone not among a group of kids of the same socioeconomic class from the same neighborhood in the same school and of the same age speaking the same language, but imagine playing it for 40 or more years, in different countries, in different contexts, in different languages. What happens to the stories? They change.

Change, he calls it? I don't think so; "change" is much too gentle a word for it. The better word for stories that have journeyed far around the world, branching out in all different directions, is that they become "corrupted," or "distorted," or even "altered beyond all recognition." (And if you're tracking with me, you're already wondering: How did such a messed-up process produce such a character as Jesus? Good question.)

Ehrman is the skeptics' best representative on these matters, but not the only one. Leading atheist Richard Dawkins echoes him almost exactly:[12]

---

[11] Bart D. Ehrman, *Jesus, Interrupted: Revealing the Hidden Contradictions in the Bible (and Why We Don't Know About Them)* 1st ed. (New York: HarperOne, 2009), 146.

[12] Dawkins, Richard. *Outgrowing God: A Beginner's Guide.* (New York: Random House Publishing Group), 16.

There's a party game called Chinese Whispers (in Britain) or Telephone (in America). You line up, say, ten people in a row. The first person whispers something—it might be a story—to the second. The second whispers the story to the third, the third person to the fourth, and so on. Finally, when the story reaches the tenth person she repeats what she has heard to the whole party. Unless the original story was exceptionally simple and brief, it will have become greatly changed, often in a funny way. It's not just the words that change down the line, but important details of the story itself.

This looks a lot like Ehrman's influence at work. There's no doubt Ehrman delivers the skeptics' most authoritative flyleaf, their best explanation for how the story of Jesus came to be.

Not Just Ehrman

It's not just Ehrman or Dawkins, though. Some authors, including Richard Carrier and Robert M. Price, deny that Jesus even existed. Christopher Hitchens wrote,[13] "The best evidence I know for the highly questionable existence of Jesus is this. His illiterate living disciples left us no record and in any event could not have been 'Christians,' since they were never to read those later books in which they must affirm belief." Aside from his mistaken definition of "Christians," Hitchens runs far afield of scholarship here. The entire field of New Testament history—conservative and liberal, believing and skeptical—considers "Jesus-myth" theory the province of fringe characters; cranks, even. Majorities can be wrong, even majorities of scholars; but in this case the "myth" arguments can clearly and quickly be shown to be flimsy. There's good reason for historians' consensus here.

Other scholars fall more in line with Ehrman (who at least acknowledges Jesus' historical existence), though they all have their

---

[13] Hitchens, Christopher, *God is Not Great: How Religion Poisons Everything.* (New York: Twelve, 2007), 114.

own unique spins on the backstory. One of the more prominent is Karen Armstrong, who in her *New York Times*-bestselling book *A History of God* dismisses almost everything we know about Christ:[14]

> We know very little about Jesus. The first full-length account of his life was St. Mark's Gospel, which was not written until about the year 70, some forty years after his death. By that time, historical facts had been overlaid with mythical elements which expressed the meaning Jesus had acquired for his followers. It is this meaning that St. Mark primarily conveys, rather than a reliable straightforward portrayal.

Like most other skeptical scholars, Armstrong tends to think the Gospels tell us more about Jesus' followers, and their late, legendary, mythical view of Jesus, than they tell of Jesus himself. Her assessment is tame, though, compared to some others'. Take Paula Fredriksen, historian and religious studies scholar at Boston University:[15]

> The impression of orderliness conveyed by their connected narratives should not deceive us about their true nature: these are composite documents, the final products of long and creative traditions in which old material was reworked and new material interpolated. As they now stand, they are witness first of all to the faith of their individual writers and their late first-century, largely Gentile communities. Only at a distance do they relate to the people and the period they purport to describe.

They're not stories about Jesus, she says, except at a distance; they only tell us about late first-century, largely Gentile communities. Bruce Chilton, formerly Claus Professor of New Testament at Yale University, tells us straight-out that the Gospels came from people who didn't know Jesus:[16]

---

[14] Karen Armstrong, *The Battle for God* (Ballantine Books, 2001), 79.

[15] Paula Fredriksen, *From Jesus to Christ: the Origins of the New Testament Images of Jesus* 2nd ed. (New Haven: Yale University Press, 1988), 4–6.

[16] B. Chilton, (2010). "Jesus' Dispute in the Temple and the Origin of the Eu-

The Gospels were composed by one group of teachers after another by a process of oral and written transmission during the period between Jesus' death and 100 CE. ... Some of the earliest teachers who shaped the Gospels shared the cultural milieu of Jesus, but others have never seen him; they lived far from his land at a later period and were not practicing Jews.

One group of teachers after another—that's who did the composing. Some of them (some!) shared Jesus' "milieu," he says, but none of them knew Jesus himself. Geneseo College Professor R. J. Hoffman agrees that the stories had nothing to do with the truth of Jesus' life:[17]

There is simply no evidence that early Christians were concerned about "whether" Jesus had really lived and died. ... The pluralized form of that datum in the form of written Gospels is the literary artifact of what they believed, not a factual record of events that transpired prior to the framing of the oral message.

Even "whether" goes in scare quotes! Allow me to translate: The four Gospels are mere literary artifacts of what early Christians believed, which had little or nothing to do with what actually happened, or even (ahem) "whether" it happened.

Marcus J. Borg and John Dominic Crossan, leaders of the famous "Jesus Project," concur. We don't know whether the stories had anything to do with reality, they say, but by now there's no point in even caring:[18]

---

charist." In R. J. Hoffman (Ed.), *Sources of the Jesus Tradition: Separating History from Myth* (pp. 118–130). Amherst, NY: Prometheus Press., 120.

[17] R.J. Hoffman, "On Not Finding the Historical Jesus," in *Sources of the Jesus Tradition: Separating History from Myth,* edited by R.J. Hoffman, 171–184 (Amherst, NY: Prometheus Press, 2010), 180.

[18] Marcus J. Borg and John Dominic Crossan, *The First Christmas: What the Gospels Really Teach about Jesus's Birth* (New York: HarperOne, 2007), 27.

A recent television special on the birth of Jesus posed the question ... are these stories fact or fable? For many people, Christian and non-Christian alike, these are the two choices. Either these stories report events that happened, or they are no better than fables. For most people today, fables do not matter much. They might be entertaining for children, but need not be taken seriously.

Thus it is important to realize that there is a third option that moves beyond the choices of fact or fable. This book is based on that third option. We see the nativity stories as neither fact nor fable, but as parables and overtures.

And what were the stories for, then? Propaganda, not truth. Take the Gospel of Matthew, for example, per Paula Fredriksen:[19]

> Matthew uses the scriptures to generate a theologically sophisticated definition and characterization of Jesus of Nazareth as the long-awaited messiah of prophetic hope.

She has similar theological explanations for the stories the other Gospel authors "generated," too.

Horus, Mithras, Apollonius of Tyana

Many skeptics say Jesus' story is just one more recurrence of other common, ancient myths of dying and rising gods. Bart Ehrman compares Jesus' life to that of the mythical Apollonius of Tyana. It's in the opening paragraph of his book *How Jesus Became God*:

> Before he was born, his mother had a visitor from heaven who told her that her son would not be a mere mortal but in fact would be divine. His birth was accompanied by unusual divine signs in the heaven. As an adult he left his home to engage on an itinerant preaching ministry. ... He gathered a number of followers around him who became convinced that he was no ordinary human, but that he was the Son of God. And he did miracles to confirm them

---

[19] Paula Fredriksen, *From Jesus to Christ: the Origins of the New Testament Images of Jesus.* 2nd ed. (New Haven: Yale University Press, 1988), 37.

in their beliefs: he could heal the sick, cast out demons, and raise the dead. At the end of his life he aroused opposition among the ruling authorities of Rome and was put on trial. But they could not kill his soul. He ascended to heaven.

And that, Ehrman tells us, is the story of Apollonius. Jesus? Just the same old story, retold yet one more time. Atheist blogger Bob Seidensticker has a long list of these dying-and-rising-god stories:[20] Tammuz, Osirus, Adonis, Attis, and Mithras. It's all myth to him, including Jesus, of course.[21]

Cognitive Dissonance?

All this might come across as disturbing for Bible-believing Christians. It should, if there was any substance to it. It really does matter whether the Gospels are true! But there's one more step in the skeptics' backstory that needs filling in. We've seen how they think the fable grew up, but where were the stories born? What got them launched to begin with?

It's a story first hinted at by Hermann Samuel Reimarus (1694–1768). Skepticism like his was so frowned upon in that day, he didn't consider it safe to have his views published until after his own death. According to Bart Ehrman, again,[22] Reimarus didn't believe Jesus had come to teach new spiritual truth. Instead, both

---

[20] Seidensticker, Bob. "Jesus: Just One More Dying and Rising Savior." *Cross Examined. Patheos,* April 15, 2012. https://www.patheos.com/blogs/crossexamined/2012/04/jesus-just-one-more-dying-and-rising-savior.

[21] While it's not essential to the case I'm making here, I should note that these myths are easily debunked. The earliest evidence we have for Mithras comes after Jesus, which makes it hard to show Jesus was copied from him. And David Marshall shows Ehrman's error with Apollonius of Tyana, in "Was the Story of Jesus Borrowed From Pagan Myth?" *The Stream,* December 13, 2016. https://stream.org/story-jesus-borrowed-pagan/. Similarly, the supposed parallels between Jesus and Tammuz, Osiris, and the rest all turn out to be empty and contrived.

[22] Bart D. Ehrman, *Jesus Before the Gospels: How the Earliest Christians Remembered, Changed, and Invented Their Stories of the Savior* (New York, NY: HarperOne, 2017), 50–57.

Jesus and his followers thought he was the king who would free Israel from Roman rule. All seemed well up until just after his final entry into Jerusalem. That entry was triumphal enough, to be sure—but then he got himself stripped naked, tortured, and executed, bringing his "kingship" to a brutal, humiliating end.

The disciples were devastated over it. "How could they not be?" asks Ehrman, relating Reimarus's views. "They had left their homes, their families, and their jobs to follow this false, crucified messiah." And now what were they going to do? They wanted to think of Jesus as king, but he certainly hadn't come through for them. He was dead! So his followers altered the message. Whereas before they'd preached Jesus as an earthly king, now they had to preach him as a spiritual one—so they re-wrote the story to make it look as if Jesus had intended that all along. As Ehrman tells it, "The disciples ... invented the idea of a spiritual messiah whose death and resurrection brought salvation." Boom, here comes your resurrected Jesus, just like that!

Now before you brush that off as, "Phah! No one would ever make up a story like that, just to save their view of a king!" we actually do know of cases where people have done almost exactly that. It's a fascinating human phenomenon, called "cognitive dissonance reduction." It's real, and it can lead people to some very crazy conclusions.

As an undergrad I read the engrossing 1956 study *When Prophecy Fails* by Leon Festinger, Henry Riecken, and Stanley Schlachter. It's a true story centered upon a woman whom the authors gave the pseudonym "Marian Keech." Keech had convinced a small group of friends that aliens from the planet Clarion were planning to destroy the earth. Her group of "Seekers"—and only those Seekers—would be saved. All they had to do was gather together and wait at midnight of the appointed night, December 20, 1954. The aliens would come and whisk them away to safety, then unleash destruction.

Festinger's team of social psychologists somehow found out about this "prophecy" and the group's plans. It was a truly golden opportunity to study a cult in action, so they embedded one of their own people among the Seekers, to report on the group and its processes from the inside. Meanwhile, other members of Keech's group—the real believers—left their jobs, their possessions, and even their spouses, so they could be spared from the apocalypse.

Their instructions on that final day were to remove all metals before midnight, then sit and wait for their flight off Earth. So they removed their metals. They sat. They waited. And sat. And waited. And waited. By 4:00 AM Keech was crying. The other Seekers just looked around in stunned silence. But then—salvation! It came at 4:45 AM, when Keech received another "message" from the aliens: This little group's sincerity had "spread so much light," God himself had stepped in to hold off the destruction! They went on to spread the news to as many people as they could.

Dissonance Theory and the Early Church

And this is exactly the same sort of thing many skeptics, from Reimarus onward, think happened with the first disciples. Jesus had failed his followers' expectations spectacularly, yet they found a way to make it all true anyway. They had to, otherwise they'd have had to 'fess up how badly they'd let themselves be fooled. So just as Keech's followers redoubled their "evangelism" after her prophecy failed, the apostles also took it as their mission to spread Jesus' "spiritual message" to all the earth.

At that point, belief was bound to spread, says atheist Robert M. Price: "The more people who can be convinced, the truer it will seem. In the final analysis, then, a radical disconfirmation of belief may be just what a religious movement needs to get off the ground."[23] Atheist Kris Komarnitsky echoes the theme:[24]

> Although cognitive dissonance often does not lead to the emergence of new beliefs, we know that it can, sometimes with spectacular results. Given the circumstances Jesus' followers were faced with ... it is not surprising that the Christian rationalization arose that Jesus died for our sins and was raised (and will return soon).

So that's where the story of Jesus sprang from, according to many unbelieving scholars. Before there was a Telephone Game to distort the stories of Jesus, there was an initial group of followers no saner than Mrs. Keech's Seekers. Her Seekers and Jesus' disciples were equally unbalanced, badly enough to concoct total fantasies to save their injured psyches. Jesus' story was never about what really happened, only about his followers trying desperately to keep a grip on their egos after he'd let himself get killed. It was all for psychological balance. Skeptical psychologist J. Harold Ellens diagnoses it:[25]

> Such narrative constructs, theological formulations, ritual processes, liturgies, and transcendental visions of reality as our fashioned in the Jesus story, are fixed upon by such a charismatic leader as Jesus or by a culture or community in large part because of the psychological needs that these formulations and processes instill. They fill these needs by giving meaning, identity, and consolation to that person, community, and culture. These formulations and community visions derive their warrant from the

---

[23] Barker, D. "Did Jesus Really Rise From the Dead?" http://ffrf.org/legacy/about/bybarker/rise.php.

[24] K.D. Komarnitsky, *Doubting Jesus' Resurrection: What Happened in the Black Box?* (Stone Arrow Books, 2009), Kindle loc. 1037.

[25] J.H. Ellens, "Jesus' Apocalyptic Vision and the Psychodynamics of Delusion," in *Sources of the Jesus Tradition: Separating History from Myth*, edited by R.J. Hoffman, 213–255 (Amherst, NY: Prometheus Press, 2010), 218.

degree to which they meet those individual and communal psychological needs.

"Psychological needs," he repeats. That's where the stories get their "warrant." Not from whether they're true or not. Truth has nothing to do with it.

This does not bode well for the quality of a story's main character.

Corrupting Processes

Let's pause now and take stock of where we are. In Part One we looked in detail at the story of Jesus. I hope you've still got the unparalleled magnificence of his character in mind. Now, in Part Two, we're looking at another story: the skeptics' version of the Gospels' flyleaf, or, how they think the Jesus story came to be. Obviously, someone's got the wrong picture of Jesus here, either the believer or the skeptic—but which one? For skeptics, the answer is clear. Jesus' story can't be true because there are miracles in it. Miracles, and contradictions, too.

That's definitely skeptics' top issue: Miracles can't happen. That's all we need to know, in order to be assured the Gospels must be fables—especially the part about the resurrection. Many will say miracles *can't* happen; they're impossible in the very nature of things. Therefore, none of the miracle accounts could possibly be real—again, especially the resurrection. And of course, if the skeptics are right about miracles being impossible, then they're also right about the miracle stories being false. Except their reasoning on this is faulty.

They take two approaches toward reaching this conclusion, typically.[26] One is to say that we know from universal human ex-

---

[26] This explanation of the problem with miracles is necessarily brief. For more, see C. S. Lewis, *Miracles,* 1947 (New York: HarperOne, 1996), especially chapter 3; or Craig S. Keener, *Miracles: The Credibility of the New Testament Accounts* (Grand Rapids: Baker Academic, 2011).

perience that miracles don't happen. C. S. Lewis deftly punctured that line of thinking:

> Now of course we must agree ... that if there is absolutely 'uniform experience' against miracles, *if in other words they have never happened,* why then they never have. Unfortunately, we know the experience against them to be uniform only if we know that all the reports of them are false. And we can know all the reports to be false only if we know already that miracles have never happened. In fact, we are arguing in a circle.[27]

Did you catch that? The reason we "know" miracle reports in the Gospels aren't true is because we know miracles don't happen. And one key reason we know miracles don't happen is because we know the miracle reports in the Gospels aren't true. Ring-around-the-rosie!

Skeptics' second common approach to denying miracles goes like this: "The laws of nature do not allow exceptions; therefore miracles can't happen, therefore the Gospels aren't true." But this, too, is circular reasoning, and thus logically fallacious. The boils down to denying God's miracles because they know there's no God, and knowing there's no God because they deny his miracles. Pockets-full-of-posies![28]

There just isn't any sound basis for saying the Gospels must be false merely because they contain miracle stories. That's getting it backwards. We must start by asking if the Gospels are true. If they are, then miracles are possible. If they aren't, there's no reason to believe any of it. The question of miracles is really the question of the Christian God himself. If he is real, then miracles can be, too.

---

[27] C. S. Lewis, *Miracles*, 162.

[28] This theory also has severe difficulties in how it understands of the nature of reality, but we need not take time to go into that.

The second main reason skeptics think the Gospel accounts are corrupted is because they see contradictions between Matthew, Mark, Luke, and John. John, for example, tells of a cleansing of the temple at the beginning of Jesus' ministry, the others tell of one at the end. The accounts report different numbers of angels at the tomb. Matthew and Luke give different genealogies for Jesus. John allegedly has the Last Supper on a different day from the first three Gospels. Along these lines, skeptics also say the Gospel authors got their history and geography wrong.

It's all in the details. Small ones, generally, and generally resolvable without serious mental gymnastics, leaving none of substance, none that affect any significant point of belief, doctrine, or the character of Christ.[29] Dr. Lydia McGrew addresses many of them in her 2019 book *The Mirror or the Mask: Liberating the Gospels from Literary Devices.*

But suppose there were a few minor discrepancies that couldn't be resolved. They'd have absolutely no effect on Jesus' character, which we've been studying so closely in this book, and also nothing to do with any basic Christian belief. If the character of Jesus is the forest and the Gospels are the trees, then these "contradictions" are mere twigs. Skeptics who focus in on these "contradictions" are quite seriously missing the forest, but not for the trees. It's worse than that: they're missing the forest for the twigs.

---

[29] There remain scholars who will find contradictions based on broad interpretive positions they've taken; for example, the Synoptic gospels' supposed lack of awareness of Jesus' deity, by contrast with John, where his godhood is clearly on display. But Chapter Seven in this book adds to evidence already cited from Bowman and Komoszewski, showing that Jesus' deity is in all four Gospels. Furthermore, the argument I make here depends on the Gospels' presentation of Jesus' character, compared to what we might expect if they were the project of skeptics' hypothesized legend theory. There is little room to doubt they line up much more with what we should expect from reportage rather than the Telephone Game or other corrupting processes.

TEN

The Impossible "Legend" of Jesus

The poets must in this case have been superior to the hero.
—*Philip Schaff*[1]

We're most of the way toward reaching our final conclusion regarding the Gospels' "flyleaf." Now we can take it nearly the whole rest of the way. It's still about Jesus and his character.

I've done character exploration exercises on Jesus with groups at conferences, in classrooms, and in churches across the country, beginning with an exercise to contrast him with well-known characters from history and literature. Each time, I ask the group to provide me with two different lists. First, I ask them to name the most *powerful* people they can think of in all history and all literature—all human imagination, even. That includes mythology, comic books, film, you name it; everywhere except the Bible. By "power," I simply mean "being able to get what you want or do what you want. Or, "If you want it, you've got it. It's yours."

Answers flow quickly, and I write them down on the left-hand side of a whiteboard or computer screen: Napoleon. Zeus. Bill Gates. Thanos. Stalin. The list goes on: Genghis Khan. Superman. Mark Zuckerberg. Alexander the Great. Hitler. I'm sure you can think of others.

---

[1] Schaff, Philip. *Person of Christ: the Perfection of His Humanity Viewed as a Proof of His Divinity.* Kindle ed. Hannibal, MO: Granted Ministries Press, 2013.

Then I ask them to call out names of the most *self-sacrificial, other-centered, giving* people they can name, drawing again from all history and all human imagination, not including the Bible.[2] Mother Theresa gets first mention almost every time. Martin Luther King, Jr. and Mahatma Gandhi usually follow close after. There's Frodo from *The Lord of the Rings.* Often people mention Billy Graham; sometimes Superman; sometimes Abraham Lincoln. Then there's my all-time favorite answer: "Mom."

I write these names down on the right-hand side of the whiteboard or screen. Then I ask, "What do you notice about these two lists?" The answer: They're always completely different. In both history and literature, the powerful people are never the noble, self-sacrificial people.

Jesus' Unparalleled Power

That's not to say there are no good CEOs, honest politicians, or high-integrity religious leaders. In literature we have Superman (the early years) and possibly Gandalf. But even Gandalf admits he doesn't have the moral wherewithal to withstand the temptation of the One Ring. You want a really noble, self-sacrificing character in the Lord of the Rings? Look to a hobbit; and not Frodo, either, but Sam Gamgee, who is hardly the most powerful person in the saga.

There are exceptions to this rule, but they are few, and they're all modeled after Jesus—as Superman was, according to his creators' own admission. But is there really any comparison between Jesus and Superman? Superman flies (fictionally) through space; Jesus *created* space, and everything in it! Superman often uses his

---

[2] Some of those mentioned in these conversations have been flawed in character, some rather seriously; some of them possibly even having suffered seriously from the corruption that comes with power. It's only an exercise, though. I record the names I'm offered, usually without adding further comment.

extraordinary power to benefit himself, from protecting himself by his invulnerability to using his heat vision to warm his coffee. Jesus never did.

No author, no novelist, no poet and no playwright has ever devised a character of perfect power and perfect love like Jesus. Shakespeare didn't do it. Goethe didn't. Sophocles couldn't do it. Dostoyevsky, Tolstoy and Chekhov never came close. Yet skeptics think the anonymous story-tellers involved in the story-distorting processes of cognitive dissonance reduction, legend development, and the Telephone Game did what none of these greats ever imagined. I say that would be a greater miracle than Jesus' resurrection.

The Character Development Problem

It would take the same kind of miracle to explain *any* of Jesus' remarkable character qualities, as we discussed in Part One. Take Jesus' leadership, for example, from Chapter Five. Who would write a novel or play centered on a leader like the one described in that memo? No one! Any ordinary leader who fit that memo's description would be a tyrant. The novelist would surely focus on the people suffering under him instead. Then they'd invent a hero who would lead them out from under his cruelty; a leader of real character, a man or woman of the people.

Every great story must show some character growth in that hero. Charles Dickens ends *A Tale of Two Cities* with Sydney Carton standing on the gallows, about to give his life for his former rival Charles Darnay, speaking the stunning line, "It is a far, far better thing that I do, than I have ever done; it is a far, far better rest that I go to than I have ever known." "He whom Dickens had earlier described as a "jackal" had completely changed, with that growth and change being absolutely essential to the story.

Again, we need our great characters to show character development. Either that, or at least some kind of human weakness, such as we see in *Hamlet* or *King Lear*. Not that anyone would or could have written a story like Darnay's in the first century. Literature depicting character in that manner was still centuries from being developed. Nevertheless, readers today—standing in the literary heritage of Dickens and Dostoyevsky—find Jesus both timeless and compelling, yet without the character growth we expect in all great literature. And skeptics think that was a simple enough feat for the Telephone Game to accomplish?

Consider also Jesus' complete perfection, from the start of his ministry through to his ascension. Perfection is almost always boring in literature. Remember Alvin from Chapter Two? Perfect? Yes. Forgettable? Absolutely! (There's a good chance you're saying to yourself, "No, actually, I *don't* remember Alvin from Chapter Two." Turn back for a reminder if you need it; no one will think the less of you for it.)

I experienced this problem of perfection last year when I binge-watched the entire original *Mission Impossible* series. Please don't think ill of me for it. I was laid up in bed for a week following foot surgery, with strict orders to keep my foot elevated above my heart. There's not much you can do when the doc says you can't even sit up in bed.

I started out enjoying the show. Oh, the things that Impossible Missions Force could do! They were amazing—no, they were *perfect*. Every "impossible" mission was perfectly conceived, every impossible plan was perfectly executed. They never got it wrong, not even a little bit.

So, if *Mission Impossible* could create perfect characters, anyone could do it, right? *Wrong*. The members of the team weren't actually characters. Seriously. They had hardly any more substance than my imaginary Alvin. None of them had a home, as far as we could see on the show. Their planning center *might* have been team leader Jim Phelps' home, but then again, it might not have been. No one ever says, and we never see much more than one room there anyway. There was certainly no sign of a kitchen or dining room, where the most authentic human interactions tend to happen.

The team members had no families. They had no histories. (Jim Phelps' dad showed up briefly once, but without any noticeable impact on him.) None of them ever had a personal problem to solve. They had no social life and no friends—not even on the team, really. They acted strictly as colleagues, not as real people who cared deeply about each other. Team members came and went without explanation from one season to the next. It didn't matter who they were. They were interchangeable.

That's what *Mission Impossible's* character perfection looked like. Boring. Only inertia, and a relative lack of other good options for spending my time that week, kept me going through to the end of the series. I didn't regret it much when I reached the show's end. There's a reason they don't make TV shows like that anymore, and it isn't only (and regrettably) because sex and violence are so freely injected nowadays. It's also because writers and producers have learned that viewers want real people on screen. And for good reason: Perfect characters are perfectly boring. Perfectly forgettable.

Jesus was a perfect character, so on that principle, he too should have been perfectly forgettable. Yet the reality is exactly the opposite. History, and the continuing spread of his church, have proven him the most memorable character ever, in any story, throughout all the ages. We saw in Chapters Three, Four, and Eight why his character never grew: He was perfect from the start. Yet a question still remains: Why has he been such a perennially *compelling* character? Is there any explanation, other than his equally perfect love displayed at the Cross? I think there is: His story touches hearts because it carries the ring of truth for those who are open to it. I believe it's also because God the Holy Spirit enlivens the story in our hearts. (I don't expect skeptics to be impressed by that explanation, at least not until they, too have begun turning their hearts toward Christ. But they don't need to be convinced in order for it to be true.)

But why compare Jesus to all these fictional characters anyway? *Simply to show he doesn't fit the fiction category.* No literary genius—not Shakespeare, not Goethe, not Solzhenitsyn, not Sophocles or Euripides, and certainly not Dickens or Twain, ever imagined a character like Jesus. If they couldn't pull off a character like that, how could anyone imagine some anonymous nobodies of the first century did? It's impossible.

Scrambled Navigation?

And that's only half the problem.

Skeptics theorize the story of Jesus started in Jerusalem (or somewhere in Israel, anyway), and then took off every which-way from there, traveling through multiple hands and lands, so the map of its progress would have looked like branches sprouting from a shrub. They picture the story being altered along each of those branching paths, each branch changing independently, sometimes randomly as in the Telephone Game, sometimes with theological or political purposes in mind—purposes that differed for the various groups that handled the story along its way.

In short, skeptics propose that the Gospel stories were built through processes that were certain to distort and corrupt any message that might have passed through them along all their multiple routes. But how scrambled did the Gospels actually come out? Sure, there are a few apparent discrepancies to resolve. Small ones. But the main story? The character of its central person, Jesus? The perfect character we studied in Part One? This is where the skeptics' flyleaf fails them, especially since these hypothesized branching, corrupting processes landed not just once, in one story of Jesus, but four times, in four Gospels.

In fact, for those who accept the existence of the hypothetical "Q" document, it might even have landed five times. Many scholars believe Matthew and Luke used another source, now lost to history, for the material they share in common which is not found in Mark. That hypothetical document is called Q, from *Quelle*, German for "source." (Not everyone believes in these "two-source" or "four-source" Q theories, but many skeptics do.) The Q material's picture of Jesus is consistent with the rest of what we know about him from Mark, John, and the so-called M and L material that Matthew and Luke independently relied upon (in at least one major version of this theory).

You need not worry much about Q, though. I only bring it up to emphasize the multiple landing-places the "legend" must have lighted upon after all its varied and distorting travels—if legend it were indeed.

Scrambled Swallows?

You've heard of the swallows of San Juan Capistrano? Every year, large flocks of them flock the Mission church grounds there on March 19, at the end of a 6,000-mile migration from Argentina.[3] Let's imagine some mad scientist decided to scramble some poor birds' navigation systems, so they could never find their way home again. Suppose this evil genius snagged a few thousand of the birds, stuck them in his evil brain-scrambling machine, tagged them, and let them loose from locations all over South America. And then every one of these birds landed at San Juan Capistrano on March 19 anyway. There's only one possible con-

---

[3] There was a period of some years when this migration was disrupted due to human activity in and around San Juan Capistrano, but the swallows are reportedly making a comeback.

clusion: The brain-scrambling machine was a dud. It didn't do a thing. Nothing got scrambled after all.

That's a good picture of what's wrong with the skeptics' story of the Gospels. They assume the story went out like brain-damaged swallows, free to wander anywhere as it traveled along each branch, without any navigational guidance to make sure all the accounts stayed on course toward a common final landing spot. Cambridge University scholar Justin Meggitt says it clearly enough for us: the various early Christian groups had "complementary and competing" views of Christianity's origins, which makes it "all the more plausible" that "endemic mythmaking" was widely practiced and deeply embedded in their way of life. And these groups had only "distant or tenuous" relationships with each other, he says.[4] In that case they could have had no reliable systems for mutual fact-checking; no way to keep their separate versions of the story on a common course.

Therefore the story of Jesus would have had no navigational guidance behind it; nothing to ensure that all the multiple versions flying all across the Mediterranean would remain on similar paths, so as to land even approximately in one place. So when Bart Ehrman says, "These stories, in other words, are not so much about Jesus as they are about the community that was telling the stories,"[5] that means the stories of Jesus that traveled outward along each branching route should have been just as varied as the many communities themselves. His explanation is worth quoting at length.[6]

---

[4] J. Meggitt, "Popular Mythology in the Early Empire and the Multiplicity of Jesus Traditions," in Sources of the Jesus Tradition: Separating History from Myth, edited by R.J. Hoffman, 55–80 (Amherst, NY: Prometheus Press, 2010), 76.

[5] Bart D. Ehrman, *Jesus Before the Gospels: How the Earliest Christians Remembered, Changed, and Invented Their Stories of the Savior* (New York, NY: HarperOne, 2017) 65.

[6] Bart D. Ehrman, *How Jesus Became God: the Exaltation of a Jewish Preacher from Galilee* (New York, NY: HarperOne, 2015), Kindle loc. 1367–1380.

The stories were being told by word of mouth, year after year, decade after decade, among lots of people in different parts of the world, in different languages, and there was no way to control what one person said to the next about Jesus's words and deeds. ... Details get changed, episodes get invented, events get exaggerated, impressive accounts get made even more impressive, and so on. Eventually, an author heard the stories in his church—say it was "Mark" in the city of Rome. And he wrote his account. And ten or fifteen years later, another author in another city read Mark's account and decided to write his own, based partially on Mark but partially on the stories he had heard in his own community. And the Gospels started coming into existence.

Now recall: What happened to the swallows in our mad scientist story? They all landed in one place. What happened to all the Jesus stories Ehrman pictures here? We spent all of Part One in this book looking at the character of Jesus—the *unexpectedly unique*, yet *completely consistent* character of Jesus, a character so original it's hard to imagine it being invented even once. Ehrman and his skeptical compatriots would have us believe the stories entered some legend-building story-scrambler to be circulated, changed, circulated, changed again, multiple times along multiple routes, until finally four people finally penned the story as they were hearing it. And in all four cases, this scrambler produced the same unique, totally unlikely character of Jesus. All these multiple messed-up versions landed in one place. Where the skeptics' theory should have produced scrambled stories, it produced one perfect character instead. Their scrambler turns out to be as much of a dud as our evil scientist's!

It's worth bearing in mind that as far as first-century documents go, we have no reason to believe *any* story of Jesus landed *anywhere* else, ever. Not until later on, starting in the second century, did other "gospels" started popping up, but they are strange gospels indeed. Jesus kills playmates in one. In another, he says women must become male to enter the Kingdom of God. (You can read examples in Appendix A.) This is the kind of weirdness you really can expect from a story-scrambler. But that's irrelevant to the four Gospels. We don't care if someone decades later told false stories of Jesus. We only care if the New Testament's accounts are true.

So the skeptics have a massive problem facing them. They think the Gospels arose by passing through a scrambler, but the story doesn't come out scrambled; not unless you insist on ignoring the forest and gazing only at twigs. (Reasonable thinking can straighten out even the twigs, in my opinion, but even if not—they're just twigs!) So if the Gospels are fables, as the skeptics think, then their scrambler produced a miracle greater than the resurrection: the greatest story of all time, with the greatest character in all literature, presenting moral teaching that's changed every civilization it's touched for the better, by way of a story gathered four times from the four winds, each version in perfect agreement with respect to its protagonist's character and teaching—all through the amazing power of a scrambler.

And by the way—though the point ought to be clear enough already—the same scrambler routed the other major Gospel characters the same way each time, too. Peter is the same Peter in all four Gospels. Other disciples' personalities are less vivid, but they all come out in the same place, too, as far as we know them. The disciples even show up in pretty much the same level of prominence all four times. An effective scrambler should at least have made John or James the more vivid character, in place of Peter.

The skeptics' explanation for the Gospels tells how they came to be altered, distorted, and corrupted, and indeed, their theory is certainly sufficient to explain an altered, distorted, corrupted story. The problem is, Jesus' story isn't like that. It's as if the skeptics have done their detective work. They've produced a theory of the murder, but everyone's still alive, breathing, and smiling—and no doubt wondering what all the detectives are doing running around the place.

Mutually Interdependent Documents

But we're still not quite finished here yet, for the skeptic might object, "No, no, no! I didn't mean the process was *that* corrupted! The stories all landed in similar places because the writers all borrowed from each other in the end."

Indeed, most scholars, conservative ones included, think Mark wrote his Gospel first. Most believe Matthew and Luke used Mark's work freely as framework and source material for theirs. John's Gospel, which came last, didn't copy from theirs, but its author likely knew about the first three Gospels and would be careful not to stray too far from what they'd said. There may have been the above-mentioned Q floating around somewhere. Mark didn't use it, but Matthew and Luke did. Of course, Matthew, Luke, and John all contributed material of their own.

But that leaves us with four sources at minimum: Mark, Matthew, Luke, and John, plus a possible fifth, Q, if it existed. Skeptics say we don't know who any of these authors really were, or where they lived. We can only guess what was on their minds, based on what each of them contributed. All of them had political/theological agendas to promote, according to skeptics. How likely is it that each of these four to five sources would have reached such total agreement on Jesus' *multi-faceted, flawless perfection*?[7]

---

[7] Lydia McGrew's *Hidden in Plain View: Undesigned Coincidences in the Gospels and Acts* (Chillicothe, Ohio: DeWard Publishing, 2017) gives additional strong reason to believe the authors were not colluding in their writing, but rather were delivering accurate reportage. Her book shares a distinctive point in common with this one, which is that it, too, draws legitimate inferences about the truth of the Gospels based entirely on the content of the Gospels and some basic, common-sense knowledge of human reality.

Consider how many ways it could have gone wrong, based on what we discovered in Part One:[8]

- One of the Gospels could have told a story of Jesus using his extraordinary powers for his own benefit. That would have marred the perfection of his self-sacrificial other-centeredness. None of them did that.

- One of them could have quoted him saying, "Thus says the Lord" as a source of authority in his teaching, rather than relying on his own authority. None did that.

- One of them might have showed him being thrown off balance in a debate, his brilliance being slightly less than absolute for it. No Gospel includes that kind of story.

- One Gospel could have shown him learning, growing, advancing somehow in character. He wouldn't have been perfect from the beginning that way. But that never happened in any Gospel.

- One Gospel author might have depicted him "having faith" in God, or worshiping the Father. Never do we see him doing either of these.

- One Gospel could have shown him deliberating with himself, reasoning through alternatives, maybe even agonizing over a quandary. But none shows him responding with anything but quick, intuitive wisdom.

- One might have had him asking an opinion of a disciple, other than the well-known and (completely different)

---

[8] Some commentators see distinctions among the Gospels in the way Jesus' character is displayed; for example, a progression from Mark's Gospel to John's in the way Jesus handles himself in the trial and crucifixion. Variations on that level are to be expected in reportage, however, and they remain far less significant than those that would have been expected given the highly corrupting processes hypothesized by the legend theory.

"Who do others say that I am, and who do you say that I am?" No Gospel shows him asking such a question.

- One Gospel writer could have had him going off course on his mission, seeking a kingdom of this world. That doesn't happen, even slightly.

- One Gospel could have portrayed him going easily through his sufferings, emphasizing his deity at the expense of his humanity. That doesn't happen anywhere in the accounts.

- Conversely, one of the Gospel authors could have depicted him shrinking from the cross, even after he'd settled the matter with the Father at Gethsemane. There's not a hint of that anywhere.

The process was scrambled, according to the skeptics. The result? Not even a little bit. It appears they have a severe problem with their flyleaf. Or to return to the other metaphor I used above, they've written their books on how the story got distorted, altered, and corrupted, never noticing that there really aren't any signs of corruption there in the first place. They're like detectives building a case for a murder in a town where no one has died.

The classic author Horace Bushnell may have written before current "legend" theories were developed, and theories at his time may have focused more on four "mythologist" authors. But his questions here summarize the situation well enough anyway:[9]

> By what accident, then, we are compelled to ask, was an age of myths and fables able to develop and set forth the only conception of a perfect character ever known in our world? Were these four mythological dreamers, believing their own dreams and all others besides, the men to produce the perfect character of Jesus, and a system of teachings that transcend all other teachings ever

---

[9] Bushnell, H. *The Character of Jesus, Forbidding His Possible Classification with Men* (New York: The Chautauqua Press, 1888), Kindle ed., 2010, Kindle loc. 835.

given to the race? If there be a greater miracle, or a tax on human credulity more severe, we know not where it is. Nothing is so difficult, all human literature testifies, as to draw a character, and keep it in its living proportions. How much more to draw a perfect character, and not discolor it fatally by marks from the imperfection of the biographer. How is it, then, that four humble men, in an age of marvels and Rabbinical exaggerations, have done it—done what none, not even the wisest and greatest of mankind, have ever been able to do?

How, indeed? The problem would be bad enough for four Gospel writers. It's far, far greater for the skeptics' hypothetical addled faith communities playing the Telephone Game.

ELEVEN

How Do You Invent the Story of a God-Man?

Only think how difficult, if not impossible, it must be to think out a perfectly new type of character, a type that has nothing in life to stand for it. It would be like trying to conceive a sixth sense. —Atticus G. Haygood[1]

Let's change gears now, to look at one more unique factor making the legend theory very unlikely. I've been focusing on what a unique story we have in Jesus. But let's not overlook that it's Jesus Christ, our Savior and Lord, God and Man, of whom I have been speaking. He didn't have to die for us. He didn't even have to show up on earth for us. No other human faced death so willingly. He set aside the privileges of Godhood, not regarding equality with God "a thing to be grasped," but instead emptying himself, "taking the form of a servant, being born in the likeness of men. And being found in human form, he humbled himself by becoming obedient to the point of death, even death on a cross" (Phil. 2.6–8).

This same hymn of praise goes on (Phil. 2.9–11) to speak of the day when every knee will bow to Jesus and every tongue confess he is Lord, to the glory of the Father. We who know what Jesus

---

[1] Atticus G. Haygood, *The Man of Galilee*, 1889 (Chillicothe, OH: DeWard Publishing, 2012), 16.

did for us need not wait for that day. He is worthy of our worship today and every day. He is worthy of our wonder, our love, our highest respect and deepest devotion. I stand amazed; I fall on my knees; I prostrate myself; in every way I am overcome by the greatness and glory of our Lord Jesus Christ.

Jesus was both *fully* God and *fully* human, his human and divine natures both present in one Person, according to the Chalcedonian Creed of AD 451. That's been standard Christian teaching ever since, reflecting and systematizing truths presented centuries earlier in the Gospels. Jesus' Godhood does not diminish his humanity, and neither does his humanity diminish his deity. This makes for a character both completely unprecedented in all literature and terribly easy to get wrong, as we'll see. How does someone come up with a God-Man character like Jesus as fiction? I can't imagine. This is yet one more problem with skeptical theories of the Gospels.

How to Tell a Story of a God-Man

Several passages in the Gospels reveal the complexity and difficulty of the legendary sources' problem, if the Gospels were indeed legendary accounts. One is the account in John 11.1–44 of the raising of Lazarus. Jesus clearly acts as God in this passage. He already knows, when the messengers arrive from afar, that Lazarus is sick unto death, although he prefers the term "sleep" for death. He knows he can heal Lazarus, but he also knows there's no hurry. Indeed, there will be greater glory to God if he doesn't rush to respond. So he remains where he is two more days, probably finishing some ministry there that John doesn't report. God can move at his own pace.

When he finally says it's time to go to Bethany, his disciples are aghast. "That's too close to Jerusalem! They're trying to kill you there!" Jesus calmly tells them he intends to do the work of the day while it's still daytime. Perhaps he's expecting they'll remember what he'd said earlier in John 9.4: "We must work the works of him who sent me while it is still day; night is coming, when no one can work." It's a simple matter of doing the right thing without fear. God always does what is right, at the right time.

Martha meets him on the way, and he draws out of her a statement that reflects directly on his deity. "I am the resurrection and the life," he says. "Whoever believes in me, though he die, yet shall he live, and everyone who lives and believes in me shall never die. Do you believe this?" She answers confidently, "Yes, Lord, I believe that you are the Christ, the Son of God, who is coming into the world." When Mary comes, they have a similar conversation.

He approaches the grave and calls Lazarus out with a shout. Only God raises people from the dead.

Now remember, John's Gospel emphasizes Jesus' deity from its very first verse. And I think if we were to try to invent a story of a God-Man, we might include something very much like the raising of Lazarus. But would we remember to include the human side of our God-Man character? John did. He has Jesus "deeply moved in spirit and greatly troubled" (John 11.33). But why would *God* be so distressed? The term "deeply moved" here says more than we see on the surface. In fact, it generally connotes anger. Following a host of scholars on this, I believe he was angry over his friends' misery and pain and especially at death itself, which even today remains the last enemy fully to be destroyed (1 Cor. 15.26). This is Jesus *the man* displaying his very human, caring quality.

Then he wept (John 11.35). He wept when he saw his friend Mary weeping, and her friends, too. He wept because they wept. It had to have been a real outpouring of emotion. John wouldn't have mentioned it if the tears had merely trickled down Jesus' cheek. He was a man weeping with men and women he cared about.

How do you write such a story? How do you paint a portrait of one person with the nature of God and the nature of man? The skeptics think it's so easy, any old legend could turn out that way. I don't think so.

God and Man in the Synoptic Gospels

Skeptics might say this is unique to the Gospel of John, the last one to be written, the one that had the most time to grow and be polished into such refined shape. But Jesus displays his deity in Mark 2 as discussed above, forgiving the paralytic's sins. Yet just a page later, in Mark 3.1–6, he is both angry and grieved over the Pharisees' hardness of heart.

We sing in the children's Christmas carol, "But little Lord Jesus no crying he makes." I don't want to spoil such a beloved song, but this isn't the Jesus of Scripture. He was too human for that. As an infant, when he got hungry, he had no other way to communicate it to Mary but by crying. As a grown man he still wept, but it was for the pain he felt on behalf of others. Just as Jesus wept over at Lazarus's graveside, in Matthew we see him weeping over Jerusalem:

> O Jerusalem, Jerusalem, the city that kills the prophets and stones those who are sent to it! How often would I have gathered your children together as a hen gathers her brood under her wings, and you were not willing! See, your house is left to you desolate. For I tell you, you will not see me again, until you say, "Blessed is he who comes in the name of the Lord" (Matt. 23.37–39).

Who but God could speak over a whole city that way? Yet who but a man would weep the way Jesus wept? The Gospel writers got it right. And no, it couldn't have been as easy to accomplish that as it appears to us now. It only looks that way because we've grown used to it.

Again, look at the famous "Come to me, all who labor and are heavy laden" passage (Matt. 11.28–29). How human is his caring here! "Take my yoke upon you and learn from me, for I am gentle and lowly in heart, and you will find rest for your souls." Yet how much his Godhood shines through: It is *his* yoke we carry. Indeed, Jesus precedes this expression of human caring with the affirmation, "All things have been handed over to me by my Father, and no one knows the Son except the Father, and no one knows the Father except the Son and anyone to whom the Son chooses to reveal him" (Matt. 11.27).

Godhood and humanity are both on perfect display, never contradicting one another. This is a Savior for us to love with all our hearts, and a God to worship and obey.

And the skeptics think this is an easy character to write?

The View from Classic Authors

The old authors saw the problem of a human/divine character better than anyone. C. A. Row, writing in the nineteenth century, asked how anyone could have invented the story of God and Man, Jesus, at his trial and crucifixion:[2]

> If the human was to be represented as dying through suffering, the danger arose at once that the artist would represent the divine as swallowed up in the sufferings of the human. But if the divine maintained its character, then it required the nicest management to portray it as not lending an undue support to a human sufferer.

Row is imagining, as I, too, have been here, what it would take for some inventor or inventors to come up with the Gospels. He called those inventors "mythologists," and points out how they would have had to write a story in which "the Son of God, the

---

[2] Row, Charles Adolphus. *The Jesus of the Evangelists: His Historical Character Vindicated; or, An Examination of the Internal Evidence for Our Lord's Divine Mission* (London: Williams & Norgate, 1868), 25.

King Messiah, could have united to his character that of a lowly sufferer."[3] Anyone who thinks that would have been easy hasn't thought through the extremes it involves. This isn't merely some good man suffering. It's the God of Abraham, Isaac, and Jacob, submitting himself to a petty Roman ruler, and then dying on the cross. Yet he does all of this without letting go of his character and nature as God.

How do you mix God and man in one character, especially if your story includes a trial and execution? Row asks that question, too:[4]

How could sufferings be conceived of and dramatised so as to have a divine aspect imparted to them? None of the creations of the mythologists was more difficult, and none has been more successful; for by means of their final drama they have made the human Jesus the Lord of the dead and the living.

Row notes that when these "Mythologists"[5]

dramatised the dying Jesus as praying for his enemies, when they represented him while sinking under tortures, as animated by the most unquenchable philanthropy, they conceived what had never entered into the heart of man before. How wide is the interval which separates this from every previous state of thought and feeling! how different from the ideals which they had been accustomed to contemplate. ... Yet no perfection which is divine, or feeling which is human, is absent.

Do you see the problem here? How do you portray the death of a man who is God, without his God nature diminishing the pain, the loss, the *humanness* of his death; but also without his deity getting overwhelmed in the pain, loss, and defeat of the trial? How

---

[3] Ibid, 281.
[4] Ibid, 282.
[5] Ibid, 284.

did Matthew, Mark, and Luke (or "the mythologists") manage to accomplish this when the idea of Jesus' deity allegedly didn't even arise until long after they'd written their Gospels?

Row doesn't believe for a moment Jesus was made up by "mythologists," and neither do I. That's exactly the point. To invent Jesus would have required genius beyond genius.

TWELVE

Skeptical Objections

Infidels are seldom convinced by argument; for the springs of unbelief are in the heart rather than in the head. But honest inquirers and earnest skeptics, like Nathanael and Thomas, who love the truth, and wish only for tangible support of their weak faith, will never refuse, when the evidence is laid before them, to embrace it with grateful joy, and to worship the incarnate God.   —Philip Schaff[1]

The case seems solid: There is no legend here. Still, skeptics are nothing if not persistent. They're bound to come back with further objections. Let's consider some of the more likely ones, or even some that are less plausible, so we can be sure we've covered the territory.

We could imagine them, for example, saying the early church scrubbed all Jesus' character-diminishing details out of the Gospels. But there's absolutely no evidence for such alterations being made, neither in history nor in any document we have to work from—which are many. We have dozens of manuscripts from the earliest days of Christianity, and many thousands from later years. Surely at least one "un-scrubbed" instance would have shown up

---

[1] Philip Schaff, *Person of Christ: the Perfection of His Humanity Viewed as a Proof of His Divinity.* Kindle ed. (Hannibal, MO: Granted Ministries Press, 2013), Kindle loc. 176.

among all of these, had such a thing existed. Yet no such manuscript has ever appeared.

And even if true, that answer would only push the problem forward a few years. It would still call for literary genius of the highest order. This person—or this committee, or council, or whatever—would have had to transform an interesting but otherwise rather ordinary leader, Jesus, into the extraordinary teacher, leader, and moral example we see him as now. What kind of genius would it have required to gather four or more accounts of this good—but hardly perfect—man called Jesus, and scrub away every trace of flaw, to make him perfect after all? (Not to mention what it would have taken to destroy all evidence of the earlier stories of a less-than-perfect Jesus.)

The Literary Genius Theory

So, what are the skeptics going to do with that? How about, "Well, if it wasn't these communities of faith after all, then maybe there really was some unknown, unnamed genius who invented it all, and the four Gospels all grew out of his remarkable inventions."

Then what kind of man must that Inventor have been? He would have had to have the genius to come up with the shining brilliance of Jesus' great dialogues. No character in a work of fiction can be smarter than the author, after all. This author would have had to have a near-perfect grasp on perfect love. He himself would have had to be the moral innovator that he pretended Jesus to be. He would have had to understand how perfect leadership requires perfect love and trust. He would have had to be creative enough to buck every custom of the ages, by inventing a character who cared for no authority but his own.

Whether it was an entire community, a branching story-scrambler, or a single literary genius, that's what it would have taken to invent Jesus as a fictional character. Does anyone seriously think that's possible? I can't imagine it. And don't forget, this inventor (or these inventors) would have to have invented a man whom thousands of people, including the fiercely monotheistic Jews, could believe was the God of the universe.

Still, when I've shared portions of this story-scrambler argument on my *Thinking Christian* blog (thinkingchristian.net), unbelievers have told me they were unimpressed. "Jesus wasn't really all that good," they say. "He didn't abolish slavery. He didn't give women equal rights. He didn't approve of homosexuality and same-sex marriage." Of course, we must remember these objections come from people who don't share the entire Christian ethical worldview.

I could give detailed answers to all these points, and I have done so in various places. I'll only repeat small portions in brief outline here. In fact, I believe there's an even more efficient answer that deals with all these objections in one fell swoop.

The Slavery Objection

Jesus didn't abolish slavery for good reason: He hadn't come to foment the absolutely massive political and economic upheaval such a change would necessarily have caused. He'd come to change hearts, a work that's had positive effects even on slavery through the ages. Wherever the Gospel has gone, slavery has ceased, gradually and without huge economic and political disruption. That's attributable in part to the love Jesus modeled. He cared for the despised and the rejected. His death on the cross, too, has often been called "the great equalizer," because he died for all, thus showing that we're all *equally human* with *equal worth* in God's eyes. This, in turn, points back to the uniquely Judeo-Christian belief that we're all created in God's image. Slavery is hard to sustain with those truths stamped on a people's hearts.

The one huge, horrible, messy exception to this, obviously, is the New World from the fifteenth through nineteenth centuries.

Slaveholders used the Bible to justify their sin to their great shame, resulting in centuries of pain, pain that still remains. This is hardly the Bible's fault, though, or especially Jesus' own fault, in view of his work noted just above. Slaveholders ignored passages like 1 Timothy 1.9–11's list of "the ungodly and sinners, the unholy and profane," which specifically included "enslavers." They passed completely by other passages in Ephesians and Philemon regarding the humane way slaves must be treated—as long as people think there must be slaves, that is. New World slavery was never about ethical shortcomings in the Bible. Rather, it was about the very human propensity to co-opt religion to justify evil self-seeking. Jesus condemned the same thing in the Pharisees he contended with.

Further, while the abolition movement wasn't entirely Christian in its membership, it was undeniably Christian-influenced and Christian-led. And though there's still much social change yet to be accomplished—our record is still far from perfect even in the Church, much less the rest of society—one solid fact remains: Slavery has never been abolished except where Christian influence has led the way. So the common factor determining, "Where is slavery practiced in our fallen world?" has always been, "Wherever people have had the means to use other people." The common factor deciding, "Who abolishes slavery?" has always been, "Cultures that have been significantly influenced by Christ."

It appears Jesus knew what he was doing after all.

The Women's Rights Objection

Skeptics complain, too, that Jesus didn't do enough for women's rights. They would never say that, though, if they knew how bad it was for women in Jesus' day, and how much he elevated their status. Women were badly misused throughout almost all of Greek and Roman culture. Their property rights were extremely limited. Their "reproductive rights" were nil; abortions happened, but they were the man's decision, not the woman's. Infanticide was common, especially tossing girls away. We have a letter from one Hilarion to his wife, inquiring kindly into how things are going, especially with her pregnancy. It includes the matter-of-fact yet chilling instruction, "If it's boy, keep it, if a girl, discard it." Meanwhile life for Jewish women was little better than for those among the Greeks and Romans, if at all.

Christianity stands in sharp contrast to that. Women figure prominently in the gospels: Mary, the mother of Jesus; Mary Magdalene; the other Mary who was sister to Martha and Lazarus, and many others (see Luke 8.3). Somehow, skeptics miss the world-shaking significance of the Gospels' report that women were the first to see Jesus alive after his resurrection. They overlook Lydia of Thyatira in the Acts, not to mention Priscilla. They're clueless to Paul's earthshakingly equalizing instruction in 1 Corinthians 7.4: "For the wife does not have authority over her own body, but the husband does. Likewise the husband does not have authority over his own body, but the wife does." And they haven't read the histories, so they don't recognize the important roles that socially prominent women took in the early church. That never would have happened if Jesus had been anti-woman!

Maybe it's understandable that they don't know all that. But they ought to at least know how much better women are treated in the Christian-influenced Western world than they have been in Islamic countries, or in China years ago, where young girls' feet were once bound up so tightly their feet couldn't grow. I've seen foot-bound women there myself, barely able to walk. (It was supposed to be sexy, their being crippled that way.) Christians in China led the way in ending that brutal practice, so that by the time I was there in the early 1980s, only very few, very old women were so disabled. Christ did them good.

India once practiced *suttee,* the horrific custom whereby widows were expected to throw themselves alive into the flames of their late husbands' funeral pyres. Pioneering Christian missionary William Carey spearheaded India's successful efforts to end this brutal custom.

Are there controversies over women's role in the church today? Of course. But skeptics need to keep perspective: Christ has done more for women than any other leader in history. Women's rights leaders in the West owe more to him than any other person. And there's more than just a little hubris in some feminists' belief that today's radical equalizing of men and women, not only in their worth but even in their roles and purposes, is the one correct answer.

The Gay Rights Objection

If it's difficult to summarize in a few words the good Jesus did for slaves and women, it's impossible even to begin explaining the goodness of what the Bible teaches on homosexuality. Issues are complex, emotions run high, and explanations necessarily run long. Some "affirming" commentators think Jesus actually supported homosexuality, and that this virtue on his part contributes to the case I'm making here. Others take it that because he was so good—and because "now we know" that homosexuality is such a positive virtue—that therefore Jesus *must have* been in support of it.

None of that is evidenced in the Gospels in any way. When Jesus spoke on marriage (Matt. 19.1–4) it was for a man and a woman. Throughout the Scriptures, sexual intimacy was for marriage only, which entails that it, too, be only between man and woman.

But there is too much on this to cover in just a short space. I've got resources on this and the other topics listed in the resource list, including my own *Critical Conversations: A Christian Parents' Guide to Discussing Homosexuality With Teens.*

One could also take a "How likely is it?" approach for a very brief argument in favor of the natural or traditional view of marriage and sexual relationships. How likely is it that Jesus, who was so extremely good on so many things as history affirmed for thousands of years after his time on earth, was wrong; and that gay-rights activism of the past few decades is right? Even for those who want to believe the Bible supports homosexuality, that seems at least like something worth watching another few decades, to see how it plays out.

The Diamond in the Sand

But even that minimal answer may be more than what's needed in the case we're making for Jesus here. For there's a real sense in which the questions themselves are overwhelmed by one shining fact: Jesus was the one perfectly self-sacrificial person in all history or literature. That remains true, regardless of whether one agrees with him on slavery, women's rights, or sexual morality. Skeptics who focus on supposed flaws in Jesus are like the man who finds a large, flawless, shining diamond on the sand on a California beach, then drops it, uninterested, as he looks around and says, "There sure is a lot of sand here. Lots more sand than diamonds. Guess that diamond doesn't mean anything after all."

The Church's Failures

Finally, many skeptics will point to Christianity's moral failures as evidence against Jesus. There's no denying we've failed. In fact, this has hit very close to home for me: My kids' youth pastor is in federal prison. My son and daughter weren't direct victims of his crimes with minors, but indirectly, we all were. For me, it's still the single most painful thing I've ever experienced.

But this book isn't about the Church. It's about Jesus. It's *his* perfection I've been lifting up, not anyone else's. In fact, that's exactly the point: He was unique on this earth. He even predicted failures among his own people, while also showing the way back through repentance and forgiveness.

So yes, Christianity's moral errors have been horrible at times, but Jesus is still Jesus. He's still worthy of our worship and obedience, even if some have obeyed him poorly. His self-sacrificial perfection is still the diamond. Arguments over the sand may go on and on and on, but we can't argue about that. There's still no way any legend could explain this perfection in his character. Jesus is too good to be false.

Summarizing Part Two, and Reviewing the Implications

So where do we stand, then, after all we've covered here in Part Two? The answer, not surprisingly, is nothing new. Griffith Thomas, writing in 1926, looks at the story just as we have done, and wonders how the Gospels could be anything but the truth:[2]

> And yet in the Gospels, written by ordinary men, not literary geniuses, we have a perfect character depicted. How did the Evangelists accomplish what no writer has ever attempted with success? As Fairbairn asked, did the record invent the Person or did the Person create the record? It has often been pointed out that if the four Evangelists invented the character of Jesus Christ we are faced with a literary miracle of the first magnitude. There is only one explanation of the literary features of the Gospels; their presentation of Christ is true.

No one has come even close to explaining this "literary miracle." David Limbaugh (the only author I've been able to find since Griffith Thomas who even hints at the flyleaf question), wonders,[3]

---

[2] W. H. Griffith Thomas, *How We Got Our Bible* (Chicago: Moody Press, 1926. Kindle ed. Moody Publishers, 2013), Kindle loc. 453

[3] David Limbaugh, *The True Jesus: Uncovering the Divinity of Christ in the Gospels* (London: Oxford University Press, 2017), 349.

Does any great figure in history or fiction possess a fraction of His qualities—this curious mixture of paradoxical attributes—what Jonathan Edwards calls "an admirable conjunction of diverse excellencies"? Is there a single idealized historical or fictional figure who is portrayed as supremely powerful yet incomparably humble? As morally exacting but merciful? As equal with God—the exact imprint of His nature—yet perfectly obedient to the Father? As divine and yet utterly human? As unfathomably complex, but simply and intimately personal?

The great church historian Philip Schaff asks, then answers:[4]

> How strange, that unlettered and unskilled fishermen, or rather their obscure friends and pupils, and not the philosophers and poets of classic Greece and Rome, should have composed such a grand poem, and painted a character to whom [the prominent skeptic David] Strauss himself is forced to assign the very first rank among all the religious geniuses and founders of religion! And would they not rather have given us at best an improved picture of such a rabbi as Hillel or Gamaliel, or of a prophet like Elijah or John the Baptist, instead of a universal reformer who rises above all the limitations of nation or sect? The poets must in this case have been superior to the hero. St. John must have surpassed Jesus, whom he represented as the incarnate God.

I love that line: "The poets must have been superior to the hero."[5] Any "inventors" of Jesus would have had to surpass Jesus himself. Plausible? Did the skeptics' supposed process produce a character better than any Shakespeare came up with? Not a chance. Their explanation of the gospels is far more unbelievable than the other explanation: that the story they tell is simply true. There's no legend here.

---

[4] Philip Schaff, *Person of Christ: the Perfection of His Humanity Viewed as a Proof of His Divinity.* Kindle ed. (Hannibal, MO: Granted Ministries Press, 2013), Kindle loc. 1847.

[5] Schaff wrote that in 1880. Why have so few authors picked up on that point since then?

And if there's no legend here—how shall I say this most simply?—then there's no legend here! There's no legend in the accounts of Jesus' miraculous birth. No legend in the stories of his miracles. No legend in his death, none in his resurrection, none in his ascension to heaven, and none in the teachings he gave. The Gospels tell the truth, because they came from people who knew Jesus, who (2 Pet. 1.16) did not make up "cleverly devised tales."

There's really just one good explanation for Jesus' character: *no one* made him up. No one could have. The stories must be true accounts of the real life lived by the most extraordinary person ever. He's too good to be false.

PART THREE

Jesus, No Matter What

THIRTEEN

How Jesus Became So Easy to Take for Granted

Yet we still find it easy to take Jesus' story for granted. Not everyone, of course. The two great exceptions lie on two extremes: those who know and love him well, and those who have no idea who he is. Between them lie the great mass of people, Christians and unbelievers alike, who find Jesus easy to pass by, in different ways and to different degrees.

I trust by now you've assessed where you stand on that. You've seen that Jesus is unique in more ways than most of us have noticed. You've seen how far beyond compare his earthly life was; how he proved his goodness and greatness in ways few of us have noticed before. For all this, I remain very sure I've left out more than I've included, and that I, like all his followers, will be learning more of it for the rest of my life and on into eternity. He is worth all our worship and obedience, no matter what.

So we've got much to learn, but we have some *unlearning* to do, too. Our culture is confused about Christ. I can't speak here to all of these currents of Western thought, but I want to touch on some highlights of what's happened over the years. It's always helpful to understand where we've come from, so we can know better where we are, how we got here, and whether we're on the right path.

How the Western World Became Too Used to Jesus

I can only speak to happenings in the Western world: Europe and its cultural descendants. It's the world I know best, and it may also be where people are most prone to missing Jesus' uniqueness by taking him for granted. Believers make that mistake much less often where Christianity is a more recent introduction and is growing like wildfire, as in much of the global South, or where Christians come under severe persecution, as in China, the Islamic world, and parts of India.

Christianity seems both old and unthreatening, here in the West, at least until very recently. For most of the past several centuries, it's been easy to be a perfectly respectable Christian here. In fact, it's been hard to be a perfectly respectable person without being at least nominally a believer in Christ. That was especially true in medieval to early modern Europe, but also in America from its settling until the past couple dozen years or so.

It was safe being a Christian. It still is, for the most part, although considerably less so than it was in my youth. Such safety is one great ingredient in a formula toward making Christianity seem normal, nothing special, easy to take for granted. But safety isn't the only explanation for it. Several streams have converged across the past few hundred years to make Jesus seem not so much *perfect* as *perfectly irrelevant*. The skeptical challenges covered in Part Two have contributed to that. Two other streams are also worth mentioning, though I must keep this brief.

The Enlightenment and the Scientific Revolution

We could go back as far as the Enlightenment, when heavily secularized French philosophers (*les philosophes*) sought to throw off the "bonds" of religion and build human future on "reason" instead. That was proud and nasty propaganda on their part, for the Medieval age they scorned so severely had actually been an intensely *reasoning* time in European history. That historical reality has been lost to many of us who've been conditioned to think of "Dark Ages" when believers all obeyed the Church mindlessly, everyone thought the world was flat, and the Church was doing its very best to stop science in its tracks. None of that is remotely true,[1] but the writers who so arrogantly named their own movement the Enlightenment had a stake in making the previous era look very dark. And the "darkness" they were most eager to "enlighten" was religion. With reason as guide, they thought, revelation was no longer necessary or useful.

Not long after that came the Scientific Revolution, which was originally kicked off by Christians. (Too few know that today.) Setting aside the much less-known *first* scientific revolution a few centuries earlier, based largely at the cathedral in Chartres,[2] there's also a long list of believers deeply involved in the founding of modern science: Copernicus, Brahe, Galileo, Kepler, Boyle, Lavoisier, Faraday, Maxwell, and many others. Indeed, many of the earliest scientists were members of the clergy. People who take the Church's controversy with Galileo as an example of its "opposition to science" have a rather serious problem: There is no second example. He's the only one. And there were other factors in that dispute, more political than scientific, that we need not get into here. Even Isaac Newton, still widely considered the greatest scientist of all time, wrote much more on theology than he did on science (though he can't be counted as a believing Christian, for his theology was unorthodox).

For many who do not know that history, though, the growth of science has always meant the retreat of religion, as God be-

---

[1] Even Wikipedia will give you a good—and entertaining—history of the myth that people believed in a flat earth.

[2] See Hannam, James, *The Genesis of Science: How the Christian Middle Ages Launched the Scientific Revolution* (Washington, D.C: Regnery Publishing, 2011).

came less and less necessary to explain the world we live in. Meanwhile, the scope of what counted as important and valued knowledge began to narrow and retract, to include *only* what science could study. Science produced results, after all. Steam engines. Agricultural improvements. Electricity. Anesthesia. Timepieces and navigational tools, which often went together. Theology wasn't so, well, *productive*.

From the Enlightenment onward, then, religion seemed on retreat, especially on the Continent. But the real blow was dealt by a pair of nineteenth century American writers, Andrew Dickson White and John William Draper, who set out quite intentionally to create a "history of warfare" between science and religion.[3] By "create," I mean they literally made up this "history." They invented it for the pointed purpose of attacking religion. In fact, the much-ballyhooed conflict between faith and science has never been anything but a myth, but they wrote that "history" anyway, spinning false facts out of nonexistent events. To real historians of science who recognize this, it's a mystery that the false "warfare" narrative still survives. Nevertheless, it persists, continuing to make Christianity look both stupid and irrelevant to those unable to look past the propaganda.

Still the God of Christianity might have remained ascendant in the West if not for Charles Darwin, who supposedly showed the world God was irrelevant to the origins of the natural world. Richard Dawkins wrote in 1996 that Darwin and his theory of evolution had "made it possible to be an intellectually fulfilled atheist." Darwin certainly hadn't disproved God, but he did convince the vast majority of the world that God wasn't needed any

---

[3] See Lindberg, David C, and Ronald L Numbers. "Beyond War and Peace: A Reappraisal of the Encounter between Christianity and Science." *Studies in the History of Science and Christianity. The American Scientific Affiliation, n.d.* https://www.asa3.org/ASA/PSCF/1987/PSCF9-87Lindberg.html.

longer. Science became the one route to knowledge, explaining and producing its highly impressive results without any reference to him. It brought us undeniable progress, whereas God was becoming (so it seemed) merely outdated.

The great problem with that, though—besides the false propaganda that's been a great part of that story—is that while science is great for understanding the natural world, not everything is purely natural. God certainly isn't. And human beings are natural/spiritual hybrids, according to Christian belief, and sound philosophy as well,[4] for we bear the image of God. Therefore, science doesn't have what it takes to access all knowledge about what it means to be human. Science hasn't even come close to explaining the most fundamental facts of humanness: consciousness, rationality, free will, purpose, meaning, even thought itself.

Science is certainly a superb tool for many endeavors, but it's foolish to count on it as the one source of all knowledge. In particular, it offers little to advance our wisdom—except maybe to give us harder problems for wisdom to wrestle with. Still, it's as though there's a numbing fog permeating the air, leading the world to believe that science gives us real knowledge, while religion has only "faith."

Positioning the Gospels as One (Bad) Truth Among Many

Our world has also seen a strong assault on the idea that Jesus is the one truth. His way might be *one* true way, it's said, but surely,

---

[4]One of the best sources on this, surprisingly, was written by an atheist: Thomas Nagel, in his *Mind and Cosmos: Why the Materialist Neo-Darwinian Conception of Nature Is Almost Certainly False*. New York: Oxford University Press, 2012. Nagel shows how the usual atheistic-scientific explanations are nonsense. Not wanting to believe in a God, however (he's said that quite plainly), he's opted for another answer: something else. That's it. "Something else" explains the human experience. He has no idea what the something else might be. Still he's hopeful: maybe someday we'll discover what it is. As long as it isn't God; he doesn't *want* it to be God.

it must be *one among many*. Many years ago, the Western world could have thought Christianity was the one true religion, but world travel, commerce, and communication introduced us to Islam, Hinduism, and Buddhism, along with other less prominent belief systems. This growing awareness of world religions traces back to the late nineteenth century, but the pluralism it unfolds received a huge boost during and after World War I. Until that war, Europe could consider itself the world's superior Christian civilization. When those "superior Christian nations" all started shooting at each other, that conceit became harder to sustain. The influx of alternate ideas has only grown in the century since then. Thus, while one could still hold that Jesus is *one way* to God, his importance in our culture's mind has decreased greatly amidst all his competition. Few now would think there is any one true way, whether that way is Jesus or any other.

Meanwhile, the concept of truth itself has also suffered mightily. There is no "truth itself" anymore, in the minds of many. Truth is a matter of choice, not of reality. Christianity is downright evil, many would say, for maintaining its claim on one unique truth about God, and it gets even worse when we extend that claim to *moral* truth, including our counter-cultural biblical positions on marriage and morality.

Our culture wants to re-make the faith into its mold. Jesus never let others have that much power over him, though, and he's not about to start now. Christianity now stands in opposition to contemporary moral culture.

Two Problems

So between the skeptical currents we studied in Part Two, the false but influential idea that Christianity is opposed to science, and the rise of pluralism, Christianity has lately seemed more and more irrelevant. We'll address the latter two issues as we move into Part Three. Having done that, we'll have the stage finally set to answer one final, crucial question: How do we recover proper worship and awe toward our Savior? Or, how can we grow beyond taking his story for granted?

FOURTEEN

Jesus Alone, Faith Alone

Christ stands ... solitary and alone among all the heroes of history, and presents to us an insolvable problem, unless we admit him to be more than man, even the eternal Son of God. —Philip Schaff[1]

Not long ago in an online conversation, a skeptic admonished me, "Whatever else you might think about life, it's foolish to pin your whole hopes on a man who lived 2,000 years ago and died young." I wrote him, "Don't be so quick to dismiss the one man who lived the only perfect human life that's ever been lived." He didn't answer, so that was the end of that discussion.

I get his objection, though, in a way. Think of it from his point of view. Christianity centers around one individual, a man who lived a very long time ago, in a remote part of the world (for most of us). His ways were simple. He walked dusty roads, wearing the ordinary sandals and robe of the common person. He raised no army and wrote no philosophy; instead, for a few short years he gathered a small band of followers, none of whom had anything special going for them, either. He taught with common words

---

[1] Schaff, Philip, *Person of Christ: the Perfection of His Humanity Viewed as a Proof of His Divinity*, Kindle ed. (Hannibal, MO: Granted Ministries Press, 2013), Kindle loc. 565.

and everyday images. Somehow, he gained a reputation for being a worker of miracles, and created a bit of a stir in the process. Far from winning him great influence at the time, though, his works and his words annoyed the local people of power. So they had him executed at the young age of thirty-three.

And now, two thousand years later, we believe that all human history, all human destiny, indeed the life of every single individual who's ever lived, rests entirely on this one young man's shoulders and his alone, now and throughout all eternity.

Imagine hearing that for the first time. Wouldn't it seem outrageous? What kind of man could bear that much weight—every person's fate, for all history and even beyond? This is way too far beyond any individual's capacity. The one who would shoulder that kind of weight would have to be far more than extraordinary— spectacularly more, even. That's who Christ would have to be, for us to have any reason to follow him at all.

And by this point in this book it should be clear—so much more than ever before—how perfectly he meets that test. How extraordinary would someone have to be to carry that weight? As extraordinary as Jesus—especially when we introduce the best part of all into the discussion: his death and resurrection. The Gospels are not legend, as we've established. Therefore, Jesus' death and resurrection aren't legend, either. They really happened. These are the core facts that answer the question, "Why Jesus alone?"

Is it arrogant for Christians to say Jesus is the only way to God? My answer: "How could Jesus *not* be the way to God?"

Jesus Alone

Let's begin with the most familiar reason to count on his being the one true way to God. (It's a good one.) *Who else has risen from the dead, once for all, never to die again?* Jesus was "declared to be the Son of God in power according to the Spirit of holiness by his resurrection from the dead, Jesus Christ our Lord" (Romans 1.4). With that being true, who could deny the authority it gives him, straight from the Father? Who else has first-hand information on what lies beyond the grave? Who else has conquered humanity's one most undefeatable enemy, death? If Jesus' way isn't the only way, whose way could conceivably be better than that?

Skeptics have tried to tell us the early Christians invented the resurrection. That attempt is right at the heart of their legend theory—a theory we've shown now to be more unbelievable than the resurrection itself. So yes, Jesus' resurrection really happened—in real history, too, not just in some "spiritual" sense (whatever that might mean), and not in mere imagination. On the third day after his brutal, bloody execution, he rose physically from the dead in victory, conqueror over death and the Lord of all life.

Jesus' resurrection caps and confirms all his claims to deity. It secures his promises to provide us eternal life.

Could There Be Another Way?

So how then could there possibly be another path to God? The strange thing is, more than half of American evangelicals are neutral or even positive toward the thought that "God accepts the worship of all religions, including Christianity, Judaism, and Islam."[2] Evangelicals do better on the item, "Only those who trust in Jesus Christ alone as their Savior receive God's free gift of eternal salvation": 88 percent agree with that. Almost half of all Americans overall disagree, however. That proportion grows even higher in the rest of the Western world.

And doesn't it just seem fairer and more tolerant to take an open attitude toward all the faiths? Christianity could be true, sure. But with all the other religions in the world, how could it

---

[2] "The State of Theology." Ligonier.org, 2018. https://thestateoftheology.com/.

be the *only* truth, even with the resurrection? There must be many true religions, not just one. It's a matter of respect to see it that way, isn't it? Anything else would be arrogant.

Christians are especially rude, we're told, for claiming Jesus is the one way to God. His resurrection is fine, a very good thing even, but why does he still have to be the *only* answer? Why can't Islam be a good idea, too? And how about the Eastern religions, which (from our standpoint in the West, at least) seem to be such grand examples of religious tolerance? What about Judaism, from which Christianity sprang? And let's not forget science-driven secularism while we're at it. Who's to say that's a bad choice?

The Cross and the Menu

Here, though, we start to see the seeds of this idea's demise. What this looks like when you put it that way is an *a la carte* menu. Religious "truth" is up to you. "Take your pick! All the ideas are nice, none of them any better than any other unless you think it is." Buddhism is nice, Jainism is nice, secularism is nice, Judaism is nice, Islam is nice. And the core of Christianity's salvation message, the death Jesus died on the cross—that's nice, too, right? Sure, it includes the injustice of his trial and condemnation, the torture he endured in his flogging, the agony of hanging there naked and bleeding, his forgiveness of his executioners in spite of it all. Still it's nice, isn't it? It's on the menu. You're in charge. It's up to you. It's optional. You can take it or leave it.

At this point everything inside me wells up to cry out, "NO!"

Jesus' death on the cross *is not optional.* It can't be. It doesn't belong on some spiritual menu of nice ideas to choose from. It's not a *nice* idea at all! I'd go so far as to say it's not even a good idea—not unless it's the *only* good idea. If it was *optional*, it was *awful.* If God could have brought us life without bringing his Son death, he certainly should have done so. But if Jesus' death was the only way for God to reconcile us to himself, as Christianity claims it was, then thank God for the cross!

For those who think there's a menu to choose from, I say *scratch Christianity off it*. It doesn't belong there. God offers no menu, no alternatives you can choose between, not even one you can label as "right for you." If Plan A was God the Father allowing God the Son to suffer and die, then there can be no Plan B. It's life in Christ, or it isn't life at all.

The Humility of Letting Truth Be Truth

Is this arrogant? Not in the least. It's the essence of humility instead. True arrogance is the attitude that says you can establish your own reality, including religious reality. Actual reality is unimpressed with such imaginations. Christianity likewise refuses to say, "It's okay, you can go ahead and choose your truth." It tells us instead, "Let truth be what it is. If you're wise you'll submit to it, even if it involves unpopular truths, including the truth that it's the only truth."

Besides that, now we know more about Jesus' character in the story, and we know that it is what it is because that is the Man that he was in reality. His greatness was in the life he lived, not made up in stories invented about him. No human on earth is or was responsible for his uniqueness; he himself planned it that way.

So, he leads; we follow; we tell the story. What else can we do? There is truth in the accounts of his life. Plenty of it. More than enough for us to accept the reality of his life, death, and resurrection with confidence. More than enough so that we can come to him by faith.

Faith Alone

Faith. We need to review that term one more time. Too many people get it wrong, as we saw in Chapter Seven. Faith isn't really "knowledge," they say. It's a "blind leap" into the unknown, with no good reasons behind it, no evidence backing it up. No thinking Christian has ever thought that's what faith was, though. As far as I can find, the whole idea that "faith is believing what you know isn't true" (another variation on the theme) originated with a couple of nineteenth century humorists, Mark Twain and Ambrose Bierce. These are not exactly prime sources for information you'd need to dismantle a centuries-old belief system like Christian faith.

Besides, if that were what faith was, then Jesus would have another historically unique trait to claim: He would have been one of history's greatest destroyers of faith! Sound bizarre? Of course it is. But that's exactly where this confused belief about what faith is takes us.

"Faith is Belief Without Knowledge" is an Irrational Belief

Let's follow a couple easy steps of logic to see why. First, if faith is belief without knowledge or evidence, then belief *with* knowledge or evidence *can't be faith*. When author Lee Strobel asked *Skeptic* magazine editor Michael Shermer, "How do you define faith?" Shermer answered him, "It's believing something when there's no evidence for it. If there were evidence, it wouldn't be faith."[3] It's one or the other, either evidence-based knowledge or else faith; never both at once. So if you have evidence backing up your belief, it isn't faith.

That takes us to the second step in the logic. (This one just reinforces the first.) If you know something is true, you *can't* have faith in it, because where knowledge *is*, faith *isn't*. If you even have *reasons to think it's true*, it isn't faith, because *reasons* imply *evidence*. Remember, for Shermer and other skeptics, where *evidence* is, there can be *no faith*.

---

[3] Strobel, Lee. *The Case for Miracles: A Journalist Investigates Evidence for the Supernatural.* (Grand Rapids: Zondervan, 2018), 54.

From there the third step follows naturally: If you want to help someone have faith, you'd better not give them evidence. Remember: Where *evidence* is (the skeptics say), there *can be no faith*.

Therefore if Jesus had really wanted to increase faith, as he so often said he did, then the *last thing* he should have done was to provide any good reasons, any proper evidence, for believing in him! He shouldn't have done any miracles. When John the Baptist sent messengers to inquire if he was for real (Luke 7.18–23), he shouldn't have done signs for them to report back to John. He should have just told them to "take it by faith."

He still could have died for our sins and risen again, but if "faith" meant what the skeptics claim, he wouldn't have dared do anything to let them *know* he'd really risen. He could never have had any meals with his disciples after he arose, not without damaging their "faith." He never would have let them hold on to him or touch the wounds in his hands and sides. And he certainly wouldn't have "presented himself alive to them … with many proofs," as Acts 1.3 says. Based on skeptics' mixed-up view, that would have taken the disciples straight from *proof* to *poof!* with all their faith instantly destroyed.

Which is outrageous. The skeptics are wrong. *Obviously* wrong. Faith isn't believing without evidence. Faith is trust, and that's it: trusting in what we have good reason to consider true. Christians have good reason to *know* that Jesus' perfect life, death, and resurrection are all true events in history. That gives us good reason to *trust* his teachings, instructions, and promises, because we have good reason to believe they're for real, even real *for us*.

There's a relational side to faith, too, which if anything is even more important than knowing the facts. Through the Scriptures, through prayer, through the lives of other Christians, we *know Je-*

sus himself. We have every reason to believe he's worthy of our trust. So we *trust* him. We have faith in him, in other words.

Besides that, when skeptics say faith isn't really knowledge, or that it's a bad way to *acquire* knowledge, or that it's a *bad substitute* for knowledge (especially scientific knowledge), it's like saying that apples aren't very good airplanes. *They don't try to be.* Their job isn't to be airplanes, but to be what they are. Similarly, faith doesn't try to do what science does, that is, to acquire knowledge. It doesn't even claim to be a form of knowledge. Rather, it's what we saw it to be in Chapter Seven: an attitude of trust we take toward what we have reason to consider to be true.

Knowledge-Based Trust

So, for example, Jesus rose from the dead, and he has authority and power to raise us from death. He loves us, he sacrificed his life for us, and he keeps his promises. But he also tells us we need him, desperately. Our sins—our moral mistakes, and our failures to place God in the first place in our lives—are worthy of death. Only Jesus can deliver us from that dark eternal outcome. We can be assured of this in many ways, part of which is in what we've seen here in *Too Good To Be False:* the knowledge that his story isn't legend, and the Gospels are true reports of his remarkable life, death, and resurrection.

So where then does faith come in? It follows upon that knowledge.[4] Faith is the response that says, "Since I know that all that is true, therefore I can trust you, Jesus, to have my life, to lead me, to guide me, to forgive my sins, so that I, too, can have eternal life." Everything in that faith statement is based on truths

[4] Some theologians would disagree with the order in which I've presented this, saying instead that God grants initial saving faith, and then comes assurance of the knowledge. I would answer that the faith we live by, following our salvation, is still based on what (and whom) we know to be true, just as I've presented it here.

we can know. It's just a matter of leaning our weight on Jesus' strong shoulders to carry us.

Why Faith Matters So Much

Having faith in him is all Jesus asks of us in order to enter into an eternal relationship of life with him. He wants us to trust that he is trustworthy, to believe he has what it takes to carry the weight for us. He *must* carry the weight, for we fall so far from matching his standard of perfection, so far from meeting God's standards for life, we need someone to take us the rest of the way: to give us freedom from sin, and to empower us to do what's good and right. We need to trust him to be the conqueror over death that we could never be.

Of course, I wouldn't want anyone to think it was enough to "believe in" Jesus for a moment or two and then forget all about it. Faith isn't real unless it *acts like* faith, which means living as if we really do believe Jesus is good, and his commands are, too. It means we respond to his love with the kind of love that *wants* to *follow* him. And it means knowing that if he is Lord and Master of the universe, then he rightly has charge over our lives.

But all this only makes sense, doesn't it? Those who say no to all that, who reject the truth of Jesus, get everything wrong about the most important facts of all reality. They get *love* wrong, for Jesus is the one perfect model of love. They get *creation* wrong, for he is our creator. They get *eternity* wrong, for he is the door to eternity, and our one true source of information on it.

To believe in Jesus, on the other hand, is to get the one most important thing right about reality. And that's all God asks of us in order to grant us entrance to the true path of reality, and friendship and brotherhood with Jesus.

FIFTEEN

Jesus, No Matter What

The person of Christ is to me the surest as well as the most sacred of all facts; as certain as my own personal existence; yea, even more so: for Christ lives in me, and he is the only valuable part of my existence. I am nothing without my Saviour; I am all with him, and would not exchange him for the whole world.   —Philip Schaff[1]

Jesus calls us to follow him. He has the authority, and he's proven himself good, loving, and trustworthy. We know he's no legend. Honestly, I don't know why anyone would hesitate to follow him for a second. I'll tell that even to people who deny his deity and doubt his miracles. Unbelievers should take a very long and close look at him. After all, each one of us gets exactly one shot at life. We could make it up as we go along, or we could choose a great example to follow—and there is no better example than Jesus Christ. No other life is so worthy of the study, so richly deserving of modeling our own lives after it. You say you can't believe the miracles? Follow his example of love, wisdom, and ethical brilliance anyway. Where will you find any better?

---

[1] Schaff, Philip, *Person of Christ: the Perfection of His Humanity Viewed as a Proof of His Divinity*, Kindle ed. (Hannibal, MO: Granted Ministries Press, 2013), Kindle loc. 188.

But that's such a terribly minimal view of the most maximal human who has ever walked the earth! Only one man has lived the perfect human life in such love, brilliance, wisdom, authority, effective leadership, and world-changing mission, which still lives and grows today around the entire world. Thus, we conclude one man is worthy of every single person's unequivocal admiration, no matter what.

No Matter What

Indeed, the time appears to be coming when we may all be faced with deciding whether we actually will follow him, no matter what. Not that it hasn't already been that way for many of Jesus' followers. I think of my family, which includes three amputees: my dad, one of my sisters, and a beagle. All of them lost their right leg above the knee. (If you think it's trivial to mention the dog, just know that when I tell people this in person, it's when I get to the dog that they really react!)

My ninety-six-year-old dad lost his leg a year ago due to his age (that's the simplest explanation). My sister Kathy was seventeen when she lost hers, the result of a disfiguring, sometimes disabling chronic nerve condition called neurofibromatosis, which still afflicts her entire body. That amputation happened about five years after she nearly died of Crohn's disease, from which she has also suffered her entire life. She's been in a wheelchair most of the last twelve years, except for the weeks it took her to recover from coma following a major head trauma, plus her months of rehab after that. I could tell more of her story, but I think you get the picture.

Nevertheless, my sister, whom I've had the hard privilege of seeing go through all this, is 100 percent sincere and believable when she says, "I fall more in love with Jesus every day." Kathy isn't taking Jesus for granted. She has tested God's goodness, and God has proved it.

Dad and Mom walked with her and the rest of us through all of this, not to mention the host of other issues that parents must care about when they have five children. That's challenge enough for any parent. Mom passed away not long before Kathy's head injury, but Dad has stuck solidly with her and the rest of us. He's stayed firmly committed to Jesus through it. He's not taking our Lord for granted, either.

Other Christians across America find themselves making different kinds of hard decisions not to take Jesus for granted. They're at the leading edge of what appears to be a growing tide of anti-Christian hostility in America, a trend that may someday force all of us to decide whether we, too, will follow Jesus no matter what. A florist in Washington and a baker in Colorado are just two among many who've been forced into court for the sake of their Christian moral convictions. Wedding hosts in New York and a motivational speaker in North Carolina have lost major income over the same. Members of Congress have suggested that no Christian should be appointed to federal office.

Friends of mine from Britain, Australia, New Zealand, and even Canada have made it clear that it's worse for Christians in those countries. Police in Scotland have posted signs threatening arrest for people who speak Christian moral truth. And still I'm only speaking of the Western world. Arrests, imprisonment, beatings, and martyrdoms still go on across much of the rest of the world. Yet these believers still believe. These followers still follow. They don't take Jesus' unique greatness for granted. For Jesus' story is great, his story is true, and his story is absolutely one of a kind. There is none like him.

Only Jesus' shoulders are strong enough to bear the weight of each person's life, death, and eternity; therefore, only he is worthy of our eternal hope.

Only one man has ever loved perfectly as Jesus loved; therefore only he, among all humans, is worthy of every person's love. Including yours and mine.

Only one man ever claimed to be God in the flesh; only one man has demonstrated the claim was true, through all of his perfections, and especially his resurrection from death; therefore we conclude only one man is worthy of our worship.

This isn't neutral information. It's the truth of God in Jesus Christ. I have known and believed the doctrine of Jesus' deity for forty-five years, the doctrine that tells us we are fully justified in worshiping him as God. But it's only been in the past few years, doing this intense study of Jesus' greatness, that I've been driven to my knees, over and over again, to cry out, "O Lord."

The book of Hebrews warns us repeatedly (2.1, 4.1, 4.11, 5.11, 6.1) that we must never drift away, never grow dull of hearing, but press on instead with diligence. Besides that, Jesus promised an exciting, thrilling life with him. The creator of our universe, Lord and King over all, unimaginably far beyond any of us in his holiness, greatness, and glory, loves us with a love far beyond our comprehension. He calls us his family; he calls us his friends. In return, he is worthy of our love, our devotion, our obedient service, and our worship.

He isn't just too good to be false. He's also too good to miss out on, no matter what.

Epilogue for Pastors, Teachers, and Other Ministers

Throughout this book, I've had the Bible's Letter to the Hebrews in mind as a model for what to include in it. The letter is extremely relevant—perhaps surprisingly so, even—to all believers today, but especially to pastors, teachers, elders, and all leaders in the Church. (That includes parents, too.) Hebrews was written to a fellowship of Christians who, while they had not yet shed blood, were nevertheless under serious cultural pressure to give up their faith (12.3–4). More and more, day by day, the same is becoming true for American Christians, and even more so for believers in the rest of the Western world.

Hebrews may have the appearance of pure theology (with various warnings and exhortations sprinkled in besides), explaining as it does the relationship between Jesus Christ and what we now call the Old Testament. That's a true view of the book, but seriously incomplete, for Hebrews is also a model showing how to encourage a church living under pressure to give up the faith. And what this model presents, from the first chapter nearly to the end, is a series of reasons to believe in Jesus based on his greatness, including a clear explanation of how faith fits the picture. In other words, it's a book of *apologetics*.

Obviously it's also filled with encouragements, exhortations, and theological explanations. But apparently the writer didn't consider mere encouragement enough. He gave them much more than that: He showed them the matchless supremacy of Jesus Christ, and he did it through the use of persuasive reasoning.

In my own book's first chapter above, I wrote, "Why would [Jesus' greatness] seem such a secret, you ask? Don't we know already? Don't we know that he is God incarnate, the Second Person of the Trinity, the one who died and rose again for us? Isn't that amazing enough right there?" I could also have asked, "Why do we need to go into any longer explanation than that? It's enough on its own, isn't it? *Why do we need all these reasons to believe?*"

The writer of Hebrews could have asked exactly the same question, and maybe he did. If so, we know how he answered it. He certainly didn't think reasons were unnecessary. If he had, he could have saved himself a lot of trouble, for he could have said everything that needed saying in the first four verses:

> Long ago, at many times and in many ways, God spoke to our fathers by the prophets, but in these last days he has spoken to us by his Son, whom he appointed the heir of all things, through whom also he created the world. He is the radiance of the glory of God and the exact imprint of his nature, and he upholds the universe by the word of his power. After making purification for sins, he sat down at the right hand of the Majesty on high, having become as much superior to angels as the name he has inherited is more excellent than theirs.

If reasons were unneeded, he could have moved straight from there through the warnings, then on to the part where he explains the new covenant and Jesus' role as Great High Priest.

He didn't write it that way, though. Instead he presents a rational, reasoned case for believing Jesus was great enough to follow, and that his way was the fulfillment of what they'd been following until his arrival. Even the theological passages served that purpose, for the letter's original readers. These believers were being challenged to think the way of Jesus was a false way. The writer laid out evidence and reasons to show them how they could know it was true instead. This is the model, a model that today we call apologetics.

If we don't see Hebrews as an example of apologetics, it's probably because few of us today would be much persuaded to believe in Christ by stories of angels, or especially of Melchizedek (5.5–11, 7.1–10). Reasoning and persuasion, however, always start from what's familiar and agreed upon. These Hebrew Christians were already familiar with their *Tanakh* (the Old Testament) and confident in its truth. They only needed to know how Jesus fit into that old message, and to be fully persuaded that he was more than a prophet. That's the question that occupies most of the letter's first seven chapters. They also needed intellectual assurance that he rightfully stands as our Great High Priest from now on, which the writer explains in 7.20 through about 10.18 or 10.22.

All of this was probably *a re-explanation* of things already told them when they first heard the gospel. I don't know that for sure, but I can't imagine they weren't taught these things when they first believed. It was probably *re-persuasion,* too, for the same reason. Apologetics is often for unbelievers, but in this case it was for believers who needed their confidence shored up in view of the hostility they were facing.

The letter took their knowledge and convictions as starting point, then built layers of new knowledge and reasoning on top of it. That's the example we should pick up from the letter: not that we should start with Melchizedek or the Old Testament sacrifices, but that we start from where our people are and what they know, then supply layer upon layer of new knowledge and reasoning, layers that supply *reasons for belief* in Christ. That's what Hebrews offered the letters' recipients, and that's what I've been seeking to share throughout this book.

Faith and Difficulties

Even Hebrews 11 and 12 serve as reasons for belief in Christ. You can be sure that these Hebrew recipients had been wondering about faith. It's absolutely central to New Testament religion, but they must have been asking, *Where did that come from? Where do you find "faith" in the Old Testament?* Yes, it shows up where the Old Testament Scriptures speak of people breaking faith with one another or with God, and also in a few passages where plainly it's important to be faithful toward God, but how often does it say *faith is the means by which we come to God?* Such passages are very few.

Paul covers the question of faith in Romans, but there's no reason to believe these readers had received that letter. This writer takes a different approach anyway, in chapter 11, telling the readers that even though the word "faith" may not show up so often in the Old Testament, the concept is *everywhere.* Faith isn't some new way to know and follow God, it's the same way the saints have always known and followed him.

And while I cannot prove it, I strongly suspect Hebrews 12.3–11, the passage on God's fatherly discipline, had an apologetic purpose, too. It's easy to imagine these believers asking, "If following Jesus is the right way to live, why do things seem to be going so badly for us now?" It's an age-old challenge to belief, one that needs an answer backed by good, solid reasoning. Of course, that answer isn't *merely* apologetic, as hardly anything ever is. But it does have that as one of its purposes: to help the recipients of this letter—including us today—maintain confidence in Christ.

Encouragements and Exhortations

But there are warnings and admonitions that come along with all this. We can't afford to be lazy. We have got to take it quite seriously. We need to exhort and encourage one another, just as we read in Hebrews:

"Take care, brothers, lest there be in any of you an evil, unbelieving heart, leading you to fall away from the living God. But exhort one another every day, as long as it is called 'today,' that none of you may be hardened by the deceitfulness of sin" (Heb. 3.12–13). And again, "Let us hold fast the confession of our hope without wavering, for he who promised is faithful. And let us consider how to stir up one another to love and good works, not neglecting to meet together, as is the habit of some, but encouraging one another, and all the more as you see the Day drawing near" (Heb. 10.23–25).

Also, "Lift your drooping hands and strengthen your weak knees, and make straight paths for your feet, so that what is lame may not be put out of joint but rather be healed." (Heb. 12.12–13). That's about strengthening each other's faith, not just our own, for verse 15 adds, "See to it that no one fails to obtain the grace of God" (Hebrews 12.15).

We don't want anyone falling short.

Doing Our Homework

Hebrews also exhorts us to be students: to learn, to know, and to understand. That's not so popular in today's church, unfortunately. When I speak on this, I say it this way: "I hate to have to have to bring up the 'H' word, but I have to: it's *homework*." People squirm in their seats. If you think mentioning the "H" word is being rough on believers, though, just look at how the writer scolded his readers in Hebrews 5.11–14:

About this we have much to say, and it is hard to explain, since you have become dull of hearing. For though by this time you ought to be teachers, you need someone to teach you again the basic principles of the oracles of God. You need milk, not solid food, for everyone who lives on milk is unskilled in the word of righteousness, since he is a child. But solid food is for the mature, for those who have their powers of discernment trained by constant practice to distinguish good from evil.

They'd been lazy. *Dull.* They weren't pressing on. I look at American Christianity, and I see how well this describes many of us, too. These are strong words. These believers should have been growing to become teachers, but instead they remained children. And you must get the full picture: They didn't serve milk in bottles in the first century.

"Therefore let us leave the elementary doctrine of Christ and go on to maturity," the writer continues, "not laying again a foundation of repentance from dead works and of faith toward God, and of instruction about washings, the laying on of hands, the resurrection of the dead, and eternal judgment" (Heb. 6.1–2). The basics are basic. We never graduate from practicing them. But we shouldn't get stuck in learning them over and over again as if that was all there was to know.

Admonitions and Encouragements

I said a moment ago I'd modeled this book after Hebrews. You may wonder where I've placed my admonitions and encouragements. The answer? Right here, in this epilogue to Christian leaders.

The church needs real teachers and real students. I'm talking about more than pastors and Bible study leaders. We need *parents* who know how to explain the truths of Christianity and how we can count on its being true. We need *youth leaders* to teach the tough stuff and challenge their students to learn. It need not be some dusty intellectual exercise. I hope this book has shown you how thrilling and worshipful it can be to "love the Lord your God with all your ... mind." It isn't just "good for you," it's really *good!*

So again, I say to pastors, teachers, elders and other church leaders—including parents!—we have both the opportunity and the responsibility in this increasingly anti-Christian age to share reasons for confidence in Christ. This book specifically follows the model of Hebrews. Most apologetics studies don't, but there's no reason to expect that most of the time. It's been my distinct privilege to present reasons for faith based on the greatness of Christ, but there are many, many other reasons besides. I strongly encourage you to make them a priority in your ministry. Your church needs them. Your children need them. We all need them.

Study Guide

This study guide is recommended for both individual and small group study of *Too Good To Be False*. It will invite you to see these things in new ways, which makes it especially ideal for thoughtful small group discussion. Each chapter has a limited number of questions in view of that, never more than six, though admittedly some of those numbered questions actually contain more than one question in them as follow-ups.

Chapter One—Seeing Jesus Through Fresh Eyes

1. Christians often speak of being surprised by new insights they find in passages of Scripture they've known for a long time. How is it possible that sometimes we "see new things" in familiar places? What do you think God might be doing in us when that happens?

2. Can you think of a time recently when you've experienced that kind of Bible surprise from the life or teachings of Jesus Christ?

3. What is your initial reaction to the idea of learning new things from *what Jesus didn't do* and *didn't say?*

4. Is there anyone close to you—possibly yourself, even—who wonders whether the story of Jesus is really true, or whether it might be mere legend instead? How would you describe their perspective?

5. What value do you think there may be in studying what skeptics say about the Bible?

Chapter Two—Jesus' Astonishing Love

1. Lord Acton said, "Power tends to corrupt, and perfect power corrupts absolutely. Great men are almost always bad men." What examples have you seen of this, if any?

2. Think of some of the most powerful people you know of from history, literature, and imagination, apart from the Bible. Then think of the most caring, giving, self-sacrificial people from that same range of history and literature. How would you compare or contrast those two lists?

3. Read Philippians 2.3–8. What do you think it means that Jesus "emptied himself" (vs. 7)? How does his example help us understand the instruction given to us in verses 3 and 4?

4. Imagine you inherited a surprise $10 million fortune from a rich uncle you'd never heard of before, and you wanted to be really, really generous with it. How would you divide it up?

5. In light of this chapter, how surprising does it seem to you that the Gospels tell the story of a perfectly powerful, completely other-centered person, meaning of course Jesus?

6. Read Mark 10.45 about Jesus' willingness to serve us and die for us. What would you say this tells us about his goodness?

Chapter Three—Jesus' Surpassing Brilliance

1. Have you ever thought of Jesus being intellectually brilliant? Would you agree that's true of him? Why or why not?

2. Can you think of a specific time when you've left a conversation thinking, "I sure could have said that better than I did"? What happened then, and what do you wish you'd said?

3. Do you think Jesus ever had that same, "Wish I'd said that instead!" experience? What leads you to that conclusion about him? What do you conclude from it about the quickness and quality of his wisdom?

4. Do Jesus' parables strike you as more *simple*, as more *profound*, or *both*? Why?

5. Read the portion of Jesus' trial as told in John 18.28–38. How do you think you might react if you were being tried like that? What signs do you see here of Jesus' intellectual and emotional intelligence?

Chapter Four—Jesus' Authority

1. Read Matthew 7.28–29. What do you think it was that "astonished" the crowds? Why do you think it surprised them?

2. Read Matthew 5.43–48. In what ways do you think Jesus practiced what he preached in that passage?

3. Jesus gave the Jews multiple reasons to accept his authority, as explained in the middle chapters of John (and covered in this chapter). Why do you think the Jewish leaders were so slow to accept his authority?

4. Knowing that Jesus backed up his claim to authority so thoroughly, what difference would you say that makes in your view of Jesus and your Christian life? What assurance, or what sense of direction, would you say that gives you?

5. What authority would you say Jesus holds over our lives today? Why do you think some people are so slow to accept his authority? Would you say this is true inside the Church as well as outside?

6. When do you find it easier to live under his true authority? When do you find it harder?

Chapter Five—Jesus' Paradoxical Leadership

1. Read again the imaginary memo near the beginning of this chapter. What do you think of the idea that these traits were true of Jesus?

2. Would you still consider Jesus a superb leader, in view of that? Why or why not?

3. In this chapter it says that Jesus never grew in his skills or his character during his ministry. How does that assertion strike you? For most people, never growing would be a big negative; do you think it was different for Jesus? How so?

4. Read John 3.1–4. What do you think might have been going through Nicodemus' mind when Jesus said, "You must be born again"? What purpose do you think Jesus might have had for saying that to him that way, at that time?

5. Jesus broke all kinds of modern "leadership rules," yet he was effective anyway. Why do you think that is?

6. What do you think Jesus' leadership will look like when he returns in his Second Coming?

Chapter Six—Jesus' World-Changing Mission

1. Other religions and even secularists often claim Jesus for themselves, according to this chapter. Why do you think they would be so eager to do that?

2. Think of a time you've tried to launch a new project and found yourself knocked off course by distractions from family, job, others' expectations, or other such things. What do you think it was about Jesus that kept him on course?

3. Read Luke 4.23–30, the follow-up in Nazareth after Jesus announced the scripture in Isaiah 61 had been fulfilled in his neighbors' hearing. First they loved him; then they turned against him. What do you think it was about what he said that bothered them so much? How do you think we might be similar to them today?

4. Read Luke 9.51–53 and Hebrews 12.1–3. Jesus knew what he was facing when he reached Jerusalem, but he remained determined to go. What would you say it was about Jesus that kept him so securely on mission?

5. Read Matthew 24.14. What does Jesus say remains to be accomplished before the end can come, and Jesus' mission can come to its final completion? What part can we play in it?

Chapter Seven—Jesus, the Man Who Was God

1. Jesus never spoke of God as "our Father," except when he was instructing the disciples to pray that way. Based on your understanding, why do you think he would have avoided speaking that way?

2. How would you answer someone who asked you, "You believe Jesus was God. Where do you find that in the Scriptures?"

3. What would you say is the best explanation for the fact that the Gospels do not describe Jesus as having faith? Do you agree with the explanation in this book? Why or why not?

4. How important to our faith is it, in your understanding, that Jesus was God in the flesh?

5. Skeptics love saying faith is "belief without any evidence." Why do you think they might be so eager to portray faith that way?

6. Read Acts 1.3. What do you think this verse might mean for skeptics' idea that faith is believing without evidence?

Chapter Eight—Jesus, Friend

1. How do you think Jesus as a child would have answered if his brothers (half-brothers, actually) had said to him, "You think you're so perfect"?

2. Read John 15.12–15. What does it mean to you that Jesus calls you his friend?

3. From that same passage in John, how would you say it affects your view of that friendship—and of Jesus himself—that he says, "You are my friends if you do what I command you"?

4. Read Romans 5.6–8 and 1 John 4.19. What do we contribute to God's love toward us? What does he do to inspire our love for him?

5. Chapter Eight says, "We want to be good enough for God . ... It's such a strong impulse, it's been Christianity's favorite heresy from the beginning." That heresy is also known as legalism. Where would you say you see legalism in action in Christianity today? Where would you say you see it in your own life, even?

Chapter Nine—The Skeptical Challenge

1. Part Two of this book focuses on skeptics' objections to the story of Christ. What value do you think there might be in understanding what unbelievers say about the Gospels? In what ways do you think it could add to our appreciation of the Gospels, or to our confidence in their truth?

2. Have you ever encountered people saying the story of Jesus can't be true? What reasons have you heard them give for saying that?

3. Where do you think most skeptics would say the story of Jesus came from? Have you seen other skeptical answers, besides those that are presented in this chapter? If skeptics were writing a "flyleaf" for the Gospels to tell where they came from, who or what do you think they'd include there?

4. According to Chapter Nine, skeptics typically say the Gospels started from psychologically mixed-up beginnings and spread via the Telephone Game. What kind of story or stories do you think that kind of process should produce in the end? Would you say the Gospels look like what you'd expect from that?

5. How would you answer the person who says, "Science has shown us miracles are impossible"?

Chapter Ten—The Impossible "Legend" of Jesus

1. Have you ever read or watched a book or show (like *Mission Impossible*, mentioned in this chapter) that lacked in character development? How did that story strike you?

2. What is your reaction to Chapter Ten's suggestion that Jesus never showed any growth in his character?

3. How would you summarize "scrambled navigation" as it's presented in this chapter? Would you say it's a fair way to describe what you know of skeptics' theories of the Gospels? Why?

4. This chapter includes a bulleted list of ways the stories of Jesus might have come out different, if the skeptics' theories were correct. What would you add to that list? Is anything listed there that you think shouldn't be there? What conclusions do you think we can draw from this?

Chapter Eleven—How Do You Invent the Story of a God-Man? *and* Chapter Twelve—Skeptical Objections

1. What do you think it means that Jesus was both God and man at the same time? Do you see any contradiction in Jesus' being both?

2. Read John 11.17–44. What do you see in this passage that shows Jesus acting clearly as God? What do you see in the passage that shows him acting clearly as human?

3. Read Matthew 23.37–39 and the parallel, Luke 19.41–44, and consider the same questions: What do you see in these passages that speak of Jesus' godhood, and what speaks of his humanity?

4. Philip Schaff said, "The poets in this case must have been su-

perior to the hero"—meaning, for anyone to have "invented" the Gospels, they would have had to be greater than Jesus himself. What do you make of that? Do you agree or disagree, and why?

5. Read the "Diamond in the Sand" paragraphs of Chapter Twelve. Would you agree that Jesus' self-sacrificial other-centeredness represents perfection, and that perfection requires explanation, even for those who might think he wasn't perfect in other ways? Why or why not? If so, would you consider the skeptics' story-scrambler theory adequate to explain even that one perfection? Again, why or why not?

The ethical issues in Chapter Twelve are controversial and complex. It was not this book's purpose to provide full and complete answers to them, just bare introductions to their answers. Individuals and groups that want to explore these issues in depth are encouraged to take them up as separate studies, based on resources list in Appendix B, the Resource Guide.

Chapter Thirteen—How Jesus Became So Easy To Take for Granted, and Chapter Fourteen—Jesus Alone, Faith Alone

1. Would you agree that Jesus lived "the only perfect human life that's ever been lived"? If true, what would that mean to you? To the rest of humanity?

2. What effect do you think the coronavirus, COVID-19, has had on that? Would you say it's caused you to take Jesus less for granted now? Do you see other Christians taking him less for granted since the pandemic began?

3. Would you agree that Jesus lived "the only perfect human life that's ever been lived"? If true, what would that mean to you? To the rest of humanity?

4. If it's true, as Christians believe, that the entire weight of human life and destiny rests on Jesus' shoulders, what kind of person do

you think he would have to be to carry that weight? Would you say he has what it takes to bear a load like that? Why or why not?

5. This chapter says that if Christianity is just one of many good ways to God (or the best life), then that makes Jesus' death on the cross optional. How do you react to that idea? Would you say it makes sense for the Cross to be optional? Why or why not?

6. Would you say it's arrogant for Christians to say Jesus is the only way to God? Why or why not? How do you think Christians might be able to speak this way without seeming arrogant?

7. Why do you think God made *faith* such a central part of knowing and following him?

Chapter Fifteen—Don't Ever Get Used to Jesus

1. Have you ever faced a situation where you had to decide if you would follow Jesus no matter what? If so, what was that like?

2. What kind of circumstance might lead a person to have to make that kind of no-matter-what decision? Do you think that kind of thing is very likely to happen where you live?

3. Who would you consider the best examples of an excellent human life: people you would think worthy following as your examples for living? What is it that you respect or admire in them? Where would you say Jesus belongs on that list of examples?

4. Having read *Too Good To Be False*, and having considered new things about his life you may not have seen before, what would you say is different about the way you view him? What differences have you seen in the way you worship him or follow him?

APPENDIX A

Apocryphal Gospels

Skeptics think the Gospels are legend even when they really ought to know what legend looks like, which is nothing like our Gospels. C. S. Lewis had strong words for people like that, in his essay "Modern Theology and Biblical Criticism," which I mentioned in Chapter One and now quote from here:[1]

> I have been reading poems, romances, vision-literature, legends, myths all my life. I know what they are like. I know that not one of them is like this. Of this text there are only two possible views. Either this is reportage—though it may no doubt contain errors—pretty close up to the facts; nearly as close as Boswell. Or else, some unknown writer in the second century, without known predecessors, or successors, suddenly anticipated the whole technique of modern, novelistic, realistic narrative. If it is untrue, it must be narrative of that kind. The reader who doesn't see this has simply not learned to read.

Note he didn't say they have not learned *how* to read. They haven't learned *to* read. They haven't read widely enough; they don't know the way literature is or the way it works. *They don't know a non-legend when they see one.*

---

[1] C.S., "Modern Theology and Biblical Criticism." In *Christian Reflections*, edited by Walter Hooper (Grand Rapids : W.B. Eerdmans Pub. Co., 1967). Available at http://orthodox-web.tripod.com/papers/fern_seed.html.

This, in a way, was my point when I spoke earlier of the detectives trying to gather clues to a murder where no one has died. They don't know the living from the dead.

The so-called apocryphal gospels (which are not gospels at all) actually *are* legends of Jesus, and therefore useful for comparison. All of them were written much later than the four canonical Gospels, by people whom *no one* thinks had any personal knowledge of either Jesus or his disciples. I include excerpts here so you can see something of what an actual, relatively early Jesus legend looks like. Remember the consensus with which Matthew, Mark, Luke, and John portrayed his character. See if you think any of this looks like the same sort of literature.

The Infancy Gospel of Thomas

The date of this "gospel" is open to question. It could be any time from the second to the sixth century. Earlier in this book, I wondered what Jesus' boyhood and family life would have been like. Apparently, someone in Christianity's early centuries wrote his own guess on that, though without accepting the discipline of sticking with what's actually known to be true. Even as a child, we cannot picture Jesus' character being like what we see here. Instead, we see clear marks of legend in contrast to actual reportage. Here are the (very brief) third and fourth chapters:[2]

> 3 (1) The son of Annas the scribe was standing there with Jesus. Taking a branch from a willow tree, he dispersed the waters which Jesus had gathered. (2) When Jesus saw what had happened, he became angry and said to him, "You godless, brainless moron, what did the ponds and waters do to you? Watch this now: you are going to dry up like a tree and you will never produce leaves or roots or fruit."

---

[2] http://www.earlychristianwritings.com/text/infancythomas.html, unnamed translator, based on the Greek text printed in Ronald F. Hock's *The Infancy Gospels of James and Thomas*.

(3) And immediately, this child withered up completely. Then, Jesus departed and returned to Joseph's house. (4) The parents of the one who had been withered up, however, wailed for their young child as they took his remains away. Then, they went to Joseph and accused him, "You are responsible for the child who did this."

4 (1) Next, he was going through the village again and a running child bumped his shoulder. Becoming bitter, Jesus said to him, "You will not complete your journey." (2) Immediately, he fell down and died.

(3) Then, some of the people who had seen what had happened said, "Where has this child come from so that his every word is a completed deed?"

(4) And going to Joseph, the parents of the one who had died found fault with him. They said, "Because you have such a child, you are not allowed to live with us in the village, or at least teach him to bless and not curse. For our children are dead!"

(Later on, in chapter 8, Jesus had a change of heart, and turned around and healed these children.)

The Gospel According to Thomas

This "gospel" was supposedly written by Didymus Judas Thomas, Jesus' twin brother. (There's a big "oops" there already.) Its earliest possible date is early in the second century. Unlike other gospels, real or apocryphal, this one consists entirely of sayings attributed to Jesus. The excerpts below are not taken out of context. They're complete sayings, as reported in this "gospel," and the sayings are all quite disconnected in the original, just as much as they are here. See if this sounds consistent with the teachings of Jesus in the four genuine Gospels:[3]

(37) His disciples said: On what day wilt thou be revealed us, and on what day shall we see thee? Jesus said: When you un-

---

[3]Translator: anonymous. http://www.earlychristianwritings.com/text/thomas-anon.html

clothe yourselves and are not ashamed, and take your garments and lay them beneath your feet like little children, and tread upon them, then [shall ye see] the Son of the living One, and ye shall not fear.

(42) Jesus said, "Become passersby."

(50) Jesus said: If they say to you: Whence have you come?, tell them: We have come from the light, the place where the light came into being through itself alone. It [stood], and it revealed itself in their image. If they say to you: Who are you?, say: We are his sons, and we are the elect of the living Father. If they ask you: What is the sign of your Father in you?, tell them: It is a movement and a rest.

(70) Jesus said: When you bring forth that in yourselves, that which you have will save you. If you do not have that in yourselves, that which you do not have in you will kill you.

(87) Jesus said: Wretched is the body which depends upon a body, and wretched is the soul which depends on these two.

(105) Jesus said: He who shall know father and mother shall be called the son of a harlot.

(114) Simon Peter said to them: Let Mary go forth from among us, for women are not worthy of the life. Jesus said: Behold, I shall lead her, that I may make her male, in order that she also may become a living spirit like you males. For every woman who makes herself male shall enter into the kingdom of heaven.

The Gospel of Peter

This gospel was mentioned by the Church Father Eusebius, and possibly also by Origen. Dated to around the end of the second century, it illustrates the fantastic ways legend can develop. I grew up in Michigan hearing stories of the giant lumberjack Paul Bunyan and his equally outsized blue ox, Babe. There's a reason this excerpt below reminds me of that: it's outsized, too. The actual Gospels are amazingly free of this kind of fantastic embellishment. Yes, there are miracles in the real Gospels, but they're reported very matter-of-factly, and none of them go against nature as legends often do—like this one, quoted here in Raymond Brown's 1924 translation. Note especially X.39–41:[4]

> IX. 34 And early in the morning as the Sabbath dawned, there came a multitude from Jerusalem and the region roundabout to see the sepulchre that had been sealed.

> 35 Now in the night whereon the Lord's day dawned, as the soldiers were keeping guard two by two in every watch, 36 there came a great sound in the heaven, and they saw the heavens opened and two men descend thence, shining with (lit. having) a great light, and drawing near unto the sepulchre. 37 And that stone which had been set on the door rolled away of itself and went back to the side, and the sepulchre was

> X. 38 opened and both of the young men entered in. When therefore those soldiers saw that, they waked up the centurion and the elders (for they also were there keeping 39 watch); and while they were yet telling them the things which they had seen, they saw again three men come out of the sepulchre, and two of them sustaining the other (lit. the 40 one), and a cross following, after them. And of the two they saw that their heads reached unto heaven, but of him that 41 was led by them that it overpassed the heavens. And they 42 heard a voice out of the heavens saying: Hast thou (or Thou hast) preached unto them that sleep? And an answer was heard from the cross, saying: Yea.

The Gospel of Judas

This writing, supposedly written by Judas Iscariot, actually came from around the middle of the second century. This translation comes from Bart Ehrman and Pleše Zlatko.[5]

---

[4] http://www.earlychristianwritings.com/text/gospelpeter-mrjames.html

[5] Ehrman, Bart D., and Pleše Zlatko. *The Other Gospels: Accounts of Jesus from Outside the New Testament*, (London: Oxford University Press, 2013).

(34b) Now when his disciples heard this, they began to feel irritated and angry, and to blaspheme against him in their hearts. And Jesus, when he saw their senselessness, said to them, "What has this agitation produced wrath? Your god who is within you and his powers (35) have become irritated with your sounds. Let the one who is strong among you people bring forth the perfect human being and stand before my face!"

And they all said, "We are strong." Yet their spirit could not dare to stand before him, except Judas Iscariot. He was able to stand before him, yet he could not look him in his eyes, but rather turned his face away. Judas said to him, "I know who you are and where you have come from. You have come from the immortal aeon of Barbelo and from the one that has sent you, whose name I am not worthy to utter."

"The immortal aeon of Barbelo" refers to Gnostic theology, in which the gods supposedly emanate or descend from one another in a hierarchy, and whose truth can only be known by some mystical insight. The biblical books of Colossians and 1 John appear to have been written partly to combat early, proto- forms of Gnosticism, which obviously has nothing to do with Christian belief.

For more on the apocryphal gospels and their differences with the canonical Gospels, see David Marshall, *The Truth About Jesus and the "Lost Gospels": A Reasoned Look at Thomas, Judas, and the Gnostic Gospels* (Harvest House, 2007).

APPENDIX B

Resource Guide

Older Sources

As I wrote in Chapter One, I tried hard to find 20th and 21st century resources that presented the same case for Christ that I've made in this book. I found none, or at least none since 1929. So these earlier authors and sources became my great friends in the course of building this study. There's majesty in their language that we just don't often find in more recent writing. There's worship there, too. I think you might find them just as helpful as I have.

Bushnell, H. *The Character of Jesus, Forbidding His Possible Classification with Men.* New York: The Chautauqua Press, 1888. Kindle ed., 2010. *Note on Bushnell: He occupies a strange place here, because his theology of the Trinity was unorthodox, and he was a major contributor to the growth of theological liberalism. This book of his, though, is one of the clearest and even (surprisingly!) one of the most devotional, in describing Jesus' extraordinary character. There are only the minutest traces of his unorthodoxy in it; traces you might not even notice if you weren't forewarned. So read this book, enjoy it, learn from it, but please do not take this as an endorsement of Bushnell's other writings.*

Canavan, Joseph E. "The Problem of Jesus Christ." *Studies: An Irish Quarterly Review* 18, no. 69 (1929): 48–63.

Haygood, Atticus G. *The Man of Galilee*, 1889. Chillicothe, OH: DeWard Publishing, 2012.

Jefferson, C. E. "The Poise of Jesus." Excerpt from *The Character of Jesus*. Thomas Y. Crowell & Co, 1908. https://godtreks.com/2013/12/07/the-poise-of-jesus.

Paley, William. *A View of the Evidences of Christianity: in Three Parts*. New York: Robert Carter Brothers, 1859. *This study by William Paley is still one of the best on evidences for Christianity.*

Row, Charles Adolphus. *The Jesus of the Evangelists: His Historical Character Vindicated ; or, An Examination of the Internal Evidence for Our Lord's Divine Mission*. London: Williams & Norgate, 1868. *Row's book is the closest I've found to presenting the same argument as in* Too Good To Be False.

Schaff, Philip. *Person of Christ: the Perfection of His Humanity Viewed as a Proof of His Divinity*. Kindle ed. Hannibal, MO: Granted Ministries Press, 2013. *Philip Schaff is best known as a church historian, but his study of Christ in this book is also very similar to the one I've made here in* Too Good To Be False.

Thomas, W. H. Griffith. *How We Got Our Bible*. Chicago: Moody Press, 1926. Kindle ed. Moody Publishers, 2013. *Thomas covers some of what I've called the "flyleaf" problem.*

C. S. Lewis

Lewis occupies a space all his own in almost any Christian studies. His essay on "Modern Theology and Biblical Criticism" comes within a short striking distance of making the same argument as I've made here. It's found here:

Lewis, C. S. *Letters of C.S. Lewis*, ed. W.H. Lewis. Revised and enlarged edition. San Diego: Harcourt Brace, 1993; also at Lewis,

C. S., "Fern-Seed and Elephants," http://orthodox-web.tripod. com/papers/fern_seed.html

More Recent Studies on Christ and the Bible

Bowman, Robert M, and J. Ed Komoszewski. *Putting Jesus in His Place: The Case for the Deity of Christ.* Grand Rapids: Kregel Publications, 2007.

Eddy, Paul Rhodes and Gregory A. Boyd. *The Jesus Legend: A Case for the Historical Reliability of the Synoptic Jesus Tradition.* Grand Rapids: Baker Academic, 2007.

Gilbert, Greg. *Who Is Jesus?* Wheaton, IL: Crossway, 2015.

Limbaugh, David. *The True Jesus: Uncovering the Divinity of Christ in the Gospels.* London: Oxford University Press, 2017.

Willard, Dallas. *The Divine Conspiracy: Rediscovering Our Hidden Life in God.* San Francisco: HarperOne, 1998.

General Works in Christian Apologetics

I could list dozens of works here, but I'll stick with the best starter material I know.

Wallace, J. Warner. *Cold-Case Christianity: A Homicide Detective Investigates the Claims of the Gospels.* Colorado Springs: David C. Cook, 2013. *The best introduction I know. Not only is Wallace a thorough investigator and a clear writer, he also includes some great stories from his career as an L.A. County cold-case homicide detective.*

Strobel, Lee. *The Case for Christ: A Journalist's Personal Investigation of the Evidence for Jesus.* Grand Rapids: Zondervan, 1998, 2016 (Updated and Expanded Edition).

See also the websites for Ravi Zacharias International Ministries, www.rzim.org; Stand to Reason, www.str.org; and Reasonable Faith, www.reasonablefaith.org.

Science and Faith

Hannam, James. *The Genesis of Science: How the Christian Middle Ages Launched the Scientific Revolution.* Washington: Regnery Publishing, 2011. *I consider this the definitive guide to Christianity's strong position in the history of science.*

Lindberg, David C, and Ronald L Numbers. "Beyond War and Peace: A Reappraisal of the Encounter between Christianity and Science." Studies in the History of Science and Christianity. The American Scientific Affiliation, n.d. https://www.asa3.org/ASA/PSCF/1987/PSCF9-87Lindberg.html. *One of the best online articles on science and Christian history.*

Nagel, Thomas. *Mind and Cosmos: Why the Materialist Neo-Darwinian Conception of Nature Is Almost Certainly False.* New York: Oxford University Press, 2012. *Nagel, an atheist, explains why atheism's usual answers to the questions of mind and cosmos cannot be true. He still avoids theistic answers, opting instead for something like, "I don't know, maybe someday someone will come up with something else we haven't thought of so far." It's educational anyway.*

Answering Other Contemporary Objections

Gilson, Tom. *Critical Conversations: A Christian Parents' Guide to Discussing Homosexuality With Teens.* Grand Rapids: Kregel Publications, 2015.

Gilson, Tom, and Weitnauer, Carson, eds. *True Reason: Confronting the Irrationality of the New Atheism.* Grand Rapids: Kregel Publications, 2012.

Gilson, Tom. *A Christian Mind: Thoughts on Life and Truth in Jesus Christ.* Kindle Publication, 2017.

Brown, Michael L. *Can You Be Gay and Christian? Responding with Love & Truth to Questions About Homosexuality.* Lake Mary, Florida: Charisma Media Group, 2014.

Walker, Andrew T. *God and the Transgender Debate: What Does the Bible Actually Say About Gender Identity?* (No City): The Good Book Company, 2017.

Mayer, Lawrence S. and Paul McHugh: Special Report: Sexuality and Gender: Findings from the Biological, Psychological, and Social Sciences. *The New Atlantis,* Fall 2016. At https://www.thenewatlantis.com/publications/executive-summary-sexuality-and-gender.

Marshall, David C. "How Christ Liberates Women," blog series indexed at http://christthetao.blogspot.com/2017/03/how-jesus-liberates-women-index-of.html.

Stark, Rodney. *For the Glory of God: How Monotheism Led to Reformations, Science, Witch-Hunts, and the End of Slavery.* Princeton: Princeton University Press, 2003

About the Author

Tom Gilson is a senior editor and columnist with *The Stream* (stream.org). He and his wife, Sara, live near Dayton, Ohio, and have two grown children, both married. Tom is the author of more than 700 published articles in addition to his books *A Christian Mind: Thoughts on Life and Truth in Jesus Christ* and *Critical Conversations: A Christian Parents' Guide to Discussing Homosexuality With Teens.* He was chief editor of the anthology *True Reason: Christian Responses to the Challenge of Atheism,* and he's the author/host of the *Thinking Christian blog.* He received a B.Mus. in Music Education with a specialty in performance from Michigan State University and an M.S. in Organizational Psychology from the University of Central Florida. When he's not writing he loves drinking coffee, canoeing, walking in the woods, and playing his trombones.

The Man of Galilee

In *The Man of Galilee*, Haygood argues for the deity of Christ simply from the presentation of Jesus given in the Gospels: Jesus Himself as evidence for His deity. This short book gives a thoughtful, thorough, and logical presentation of the unique and universal quality of the character of Jesus. Preface by Homer Hailey and Ferrell Jenkins. New preface by Dr. Dan Petty.

The Gospel of the Resurrection

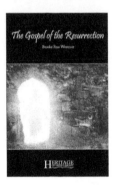

In this classic work, B. F. Westcott offers not just a historical defense of the resurrection but also a wide-ranging exploration of the significance of the resurrection for the individual, for the church, for nations, for mankind, and at the widest reach, for creation itself. "The question at issue," he says, "is a view of the whole Universe, of all being and of all life, of man and of the world, and of God." New introduction by Dr. Timothy McGrew.

Evidences of Christianity

Parts 1–4

In this masterpiece of apologetics, McGarvey writes as a scholar who is thoroughly familiar with the most skeptical criticism of his day but completely persuaded that traditional views of the authorship, historical trustworthiness, and inspiration of Scripture are rationally defensible—a position more conservative than that held by most mainstream New Testament scholars today. But the change in the sociology of New Testament scholarship has been driven far more by philosophical fashion than by any change in the evidence itself. For just that reason, McGarvey's *Evidences of Christianity* affords a much-needed counterbalance for those whose study of apologetics has been filtered through the lens of modernism. Foreword by Timothy McGrew.

Hidden in Plain View
Undesigned Coincidences in the Gospels and Acts

An undesigned coincidence is an apparently casual, yet puzzle-like "fit" between two or more texts, and its best explanation is that the authors knew the truth about the events they describe or allude to. Connections of this kind among passages in New Testament texts give us reason to believe that these documents came from honest eyewitness sources, people "in the know" about the events they relate—solid evidence all Christians can use to defend the Scriptures and the truth of Christianity.

Faith Thinkers
30 Christian Apologists You Should Know

A clear overview of the history of Christian faith thinkers. Rob Bowman engages with some of the greatest thinkers from the first century through the twentieth. Becoming familiar with the works of these 30 thinkers will prepare you to participate meaningfully in a 2,000-year-old conversation.

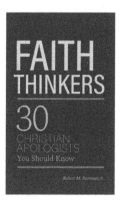

Just Jesus
The Evidence of History

Few people are able to ignore Jesus. He has devotees and detractors, but hardly anyone is neutral about him. But how much do we know about him? Whether we love him or loathe him, it only makes sense that we know what and whom we're talking about. Just Jesus is about what we can know about Jesus. Jesus isn't just a religious idea but a phenomenon of history. That means we can and should ask about him all of the historical questions we can think of and see which ones can and can't be answered. Fortunately, we're able to learn a lot more about Jesus than most people think.

For a full listing of our books, visit DeWard's website:
www.deward.com

Lightning Source UK Ltd.
Milton Keynes UK
UKHW041837261020
372255UK00004B/1185